THE CASE FOR CHOICE
One Size Fits All

An Outdated Education Model for the 21st Century

Dr. Karen M.S. Hiltz

La Maison Publishing, Inc.
Vero Beach, Florida
The Hibiscus City
lamaisonpublishing@gmail.com

Testimonials

Karen was an excellent member of the Franklin County School Board. She showed great devotion to students, parents and the community. She not only wanted student needs met, but also considered the needs of taxpayers having an economically run school system. She was also an outstanding promoter of the Smith Mountain Lake community as well as Franklin County.

Virgil Goode Jr.
Former U.S. House of Representatives, 5th District
Franklin County, VA

Karen has displayed a sincere passion for improving the education system in the Commonwealth of Virginia. As an elected School Board member, her willingness to engage her colleagues and constituents in discussing critical issues to affect real change is refreshing. Her ability to think outside the box in a system that is laden with red tape and the status quo is challenging.

Delegate R. Steven Landes, R – Augusta County
Chairman of the House Education Committee

The first time I met Karen was at the 2017 Virginia General Assembly, after I had spoken at a House Education sub-committee meeting. I was immediately impressed with her knowledge of and enthusiasm for our children's education. Her professional knowledge, depth of experience, and fearless activism uniquely qualify her to share the case for education choice through the eyes of those individuals who have lived it.

Kristin L. Allen
President, Education United, LLC

Acknowledgements

First, I'm grateful the Lord gave me the vision and determination to complete this book. Sharing stories is one way to help others endure and overcome the many rotten apples life tosses at us.

Second, I want to express my gratitude to these twelve individuals who agreed to share their stories. Their willingness to help others realize they are not alone is priceless.

Lastly, I am very thankful for my husband, Chuck Hiltz, and all that he endures by being married to me.

Introduction

The United States of America is a melting pot of differing cultures, ethnicities and backgrounds. United as Americans, yet we each remain an individual. We enjoy constitutional freedoms, rely on the rule of law, appreciate the benefits our capitalist economy provides and expect variety in our lives. These freedoms allow us to choose where to live, whom to marry, the type of vehicle we drive, what activities to participate in and whom to vote for. Yet, when it comes to education we are *expected* to enroll our children in an education system that uses an outdated agrarian model that is well over 150 years.

This public education system model, does it continue to be a useful model? Could children be better served with a different model? Might this be a reason for an increase of parents seeking education alternatives? What about the *one-size-fits-all* standardized testing? Or is there something else?

Making choices is part of our American DNA, but when it comes to education there is a resistance to choice. So I ask, "Why does the term *school choice* cause such controversy? Why do these two words, when joined together, create such a divide?"

The reality is choice programs primarily fall within the public education system constructed by state constitutions, legislation and public policy. This places the education system in the hands of bureaucrats who have a vested interest in maintaining the status quo. These bureaucrats include legislatures, governors and school boards, among others, who are influenced by a variety of advocates and opponents. This reinforces my belief that education is more about power and control of the system, rather than two simple words: *school choice*.

Let's define a couple of words: *insanity* and *education*. Attributed to Albert Einstein, the definition of insanity is: *"doing the same thing over and over and expecting different results."* Isn't this what we've been doing in education for decades? Operating under the same model, structure and processes?

Dictionary.com defines education as: *"the act or process of imparting or acquiring general knowledge, developing the powers of reasoning and judgment, and generally of preparing oneself or others intellectually for mature life."* Are our children instilled with *the act or process of imparting or acquiring general knowledge* they need to succeed? What about *developing the powers of reasoning and judgment*? How well are we doing with *generally preparing oneself or others intellectually for mature life*? Many might answer in the affirmative. Others will *tell you a story* of an education experience. Stories like those you'll find in these pages. You, the reader, must decide whether this definition of education is relevant today.

Let me state that I am not a lifelong educator; I am a lifelong learner. I do not consider myself an expert in education, but I do have real, practical and applicable experience. I came to the field later in life after serving in the U.S. Navy and retiring from a career in Federal Acquisition and Procurement. In fact, I pursued my MBA because I intended to teach at the college level, once I finished my career. I presumed it would be something fun and rewarding; so that's what I did.

Relocating to the foothills of the Blue Ridge Mountains afforded me the opportunity to teach at a private, four-year institution. My dean took a chance on me, provided the necessary tools and let me loose in the classroom.

It was a bit daunting at first. I had taught professionals, but never young adults in a college environment. In some sense it may not seem that different; after all, both environments had course materials, students and a classroom. However, the primary differences lay in why individuals were seeking education opportunities.

Career professionals sought to increase their knowledge in hopes of obtaining greater responsibility and promotion. College students were in school for multiple reasons. Some attended college because their parents told them they had to. Some believed a degree would ensure them better job prospects. Others had received a scholarship or were simply there because they didn't know what else to do.

Teaching was enjoyable, but I admit it is not an easy profession. There were students who needed to take remediation courses, as well as many who lacked accountability, time management and decision-making skills.

During these years I became passionate about education. The real eye-opener came when I was elected to the local public school board. I was perplexed by the myriad of factors impacting K-12 education, including:

1. the volume of federal and state legislation, policy and regulation;
2. the influence of and reliance on technology;
3. societal expectations and their impact;
4. a lack of workforce development programs; and
5. the bureaucracy that permeates the system.

These, along with other factors, often produce unrealistic expectations where students are not able to capitalize on their talents and realize their full potential for becoming skilled individuals ready to enter the job market.

Traditional public school continues to be the primary provider of education in America. Increased expectations and demands serve to make the system more bureaucratic and cumbersome. The ability to adapt to individuals' differing needs and talents and to align skills to changing job markets is almost lost. Our complex society and increased demands for improved methods, techniques and tools are real. Skillsets necessary for today's workforce are not the same as those of yesteryear.

The reality of system deficiencies should drive parents and students to seek alternative education environments. So why do we continue on this one path? Why are we using one method and promoting one mindset to define education success?

Parents should be the primary decision-makers for choosing the best education environment for their child. I do not believe education should be left solely in the hands of a government bureaucracy. Nevertheless, when parents do assert their authority to choose an education environment other than traditional public school, it suddenly becomes the *right of the state* to make that decision. Why is this? I have two answers: 1) power and control, and 2) funding.

Governments, unions and special interest groups retain control over the public education system. These entities control the legislation, policy, programs, curriculum, etc., which in turn control the public funds. These are the overarching arguments when it comes to discussing education. Regardless of education options afforded to parents and students, the contentious and hyperbolic rhetoric continues to be triggered by two simple words: *school choice*.

This book focuses on 12 stories illustrating people's personal experiences and perspectives within a system that includes public, private and homeschool environments. Each story reflects a personal experience and represents *choice*. The common theme is the desire to seek the best-learning environment for children. Whether that means providing alternatives or simply utilizing better methods, techniques and tools, the objective is to help children succeed. Each person profiled here sought the freedom to individually define success; *not allow the system to define success for them.*

There are many reasons individuals and groups advocate for alternatives to the traditional public environment. I point to three fundamental reasons:

1) parents love their children;

2) advocates care about students; and

3) our nation expects a well-educated populace.

I believe these stories reflect these reasons.

The personal experiences in this book speak for themselves. However, I've added my perspective based on my experience and knowledge as a sitting public school board member, educator and business professional. I hope every reader will appreciate and understand what these stories have to say. If you can identify with or know someone who identifies with at least one of the experiences, please share with them.

This book is my attempt to provide information and resources to help those seeking an alternative education environment. It is my hope you will be bold in seeking help if you are struggling. It is my prayer that parents find the courage to stand up to the system and do what is best for their child.

We are not islands!

Table of Contents

The Case for Choice
One Size Fits All

An Outdated Education Model for the 21st Century

Walter

Spiderman Leads to Education Success

Walter, a little boy from Ohio, began his education at an inner-city public school. His elementary school environment involved dealing with bullying, gangs, drugs, shootings and more. Then one-day he wore his favorite shirt to school, a soft button down Spiderman shirt that changed his life. That was the day a few classmates decided to literally rip the shirt off his back. This became a devastating memory, which ended Walter's education, as he knew it, and projected him into a world that would forever transform his life. Spiderman IS a real life hero for this little boy.

The Journey Begins

I describe myself as *not a typical little boy* and go so far as to say I'm a *bit unusual*. However, I admit to being typical when it comes to playing with friends, riding bikes and playing basketball at the local neighborhood courts and gym.

Like most little boys in elementary school, I was energetic, made friends and was overall a happy kid. However, my energy and fun personality was not a good fit in the classroom environment, nor was it expected. During the early years, my behavior led to various incidents where I would routinely be in trouble. Whether it was for talking, squirming in my seat or being some sort of distraction, this environment was not where I excelled. My behavior often led to many trips to the Principal's office along with many meetings between my parents and school administration.

In an endeavor to *fix* my behavior, the administration made no effort to adopt, change or modify teaching styles and methods. The same curriculum was taught and the classroom stayed the same. Though I did not change either, I continued to be sent back to that same environment. As a young boy *labeled* mischievous and a problem child, making no change wasn't a solution to fix or improve my academic standing. I continued struggling and my dislike, actually hated, for school grew. My attendance record was reflective of this.

With a positive attitude towards school quickly diminishing, I began looking for ways to skip school. A common practice was to *pretend* to be sick, claiming a stomachache, sore throat or something not easily visible. This makes it difficult for mom and dad to determine if the alleged illness is real or fake. So I was able to miss school, which was the objective.

Over a several year period, I changed schools annually, while my parents sought a suitable environment. Learning style seemed to be a focus, which I profess to be a visual, hands-on and interactive learner. Confident that most will agree, many schools do not utilize learning curriculum, methods and tools that include engaged learning, as in my case.

This one particular day, I came home from school with bruises, I was crying and my Spiderman shirt ripped to pieces, which was horrifying to my mother. This was a defining point in time and the situation could no longer be tolerated. It became a critical endeavor to find an environment where I would be safe, get the needed help from an academic perspective and increase the probability of obtaining a high school diploma.

It was towards the end of the fifth grade when the non-profit organization, *School Choice Ohio*, contacted my parents. This organization tracks failing public schools to inform families of a scholarship program offered by the Ohio Department of Education. Struggling students who met program criteria could be awarded a scholarship to attend private school.

My parents were a bit skeptical, but were more concerned about safety. Not familiar with the program, my mother did research in order to become an informed consumer. Upon further discussion, it was decided to submit the application, as they knew there was nothing to lose. If I was accepted into an environment that fit my learning style and would be safe, they were willing to take the risk.

The day came when my mother and I toured a private school. My first impression was not positive. Immediately I decided it was *just another school* and on top of that, I would have to wear a uniform, which was not cool! During the tour, we met several teachers and staff, but I wasn't convinced this was the right place. However, my mother gave me two choices. You can either try this school or continue to go down the same road as your friends. The friends' road was not a good road because it involved juvenile court, juvenile detention, shootouts and things that were not going to make me a successful or productive citizen.

To no surprise, the choice to attend the private school won the day. Within a few short weeks I realized my perspective about education was changing. The teachers and staff acted differently. They were supportive and wanted to see me succeed, which was a new experience.

There were hurdles and struggles along the road in this new environment, but there was a support system to help me figure it out. Teachers and staff would help with whatever I was struggling with, whether it was math, English or history. The contrast is the support and encouragement I had along the way, coupled with the determination of the teachers expecting me to succeed, even when I was determined not to.

This was the opposite of my experience in the public school system, which is similar to what other high poverty, low-income children experience in inner-city public schools. Too many are told they will never amount to anything, are constantly causing problems and continue to struggle. Statistically, many children eventually end up being a number, passed along to the next grade without becoming academically proficient. Some children do graduate, yet far too many drop out or end up in jail.

I have friends and siblings, who attended public school, that have done well and some of my siblings have goals. One is planning to work for the CIA; another one plans to own a music channel. However, I didn't think about goals until I began private school.

My perspective is each child is an individual and one system doesn't work for every child. I'm not saying private school is better than public school or that everyone should go to private school. I simply believe my experience led me to focus on the best fit for the child. It's about more than education. It's about lifestyle and available choices.

An experience I never dreamt I would have was the two weeks spent in Europe traveling around France and Switzerland. I thought this was beyond reach as a child, particularly based on my family's economic status. Yet, now I understand education is a key to breaking the poverty cycle. The proper education gives a child the ability to go out and achieve whatever it is they want.

Growing up I never thought I'd do broadcasting with possible internships at Fox Sports and ESPN. Or the possibility of running for public office, which was never something I thought about before. I've met people who have encouraged me to consider possibilities, such as running for president. I laughed at the time, but it can be a real goal. It's something to consider and all this stems from the proper education.

EdChoice Scholarship Program

Ohio offers education programs to help low-income, special education and other groups of children. EdChoice Ohio is one such program. It is designed to offer scholarships to qualified applicants for low-income families with children attending underperforming local public schools.

As previously mentioned, *School Choice Ohio* reached out to my family. This organization gathers data from the Ohio Department of Education, based on address, and compares it with schools that fall in the failing or low performing category. They do a one-to-one outreach to inform families about alternative programs.

School Choice Ohio obtains files with names, addresses and phone numbers and makes cold calls to inform parents for what is available to them. Through this effort, I received a scholarship due to the fact I attended a school with the status of academic emergency or academic probation, a performance rating of failing. Also, I had the opportunity to intern at School Choice Ohio for quite a few years.

Driving Factors and Hurdles

Various reasons or factors drive people to move outside their comfort zone and deal with hurdles they find themselves attempting to overcome. My family is no different.

My mother's driving factor was to find a school where I would graduate from high school. And her persistence paid off! She knew there was something out there for me. Coming home with ripped clothes, bruises or dealing with other issues wasn't going to be the end of my story. This was a focus for her. In the end a place was found where I began to like school, excel in academics, participate in a range of activities and dream big dreams.

My driving factor was realizing the support the private school provided. I began to realize I could achieve and succeed. I wasn't simply a number or a problem and became aware of the time teachers and coaches were investing to help with my studies. I didn't want to let them down, so I took initiative and came to class prepared. This was a mind-shift. It produced positive results and motivated me to do my best.

The greatest hurdle was from within. To have the confidence and ability to go out and do things was a challenge, because I came from a place where I struggled to be myself. However, the change of environments helped adjust my attitude. I realized the perceived hurdles were all in my mind and that I could succeed at reaching goals. My confidence grew when I saw the potential and coupled with the successes I was experiencing.

During my senior year a friend challenged me at golf. We made a bet that I couldn't play golf or be competitive because I had never played before and was a southpaw. Entering my senior year, my confidence level was such that I accepted the challenge. Whether I was good or bad wasn't the issue or did it matter. I knew I could take the step knowing I would do my best. In addition, I'm a very competitive person.

Pride was another hurdle. It's difficult for most people to seek help, let alone admit they need help. Maturity made me realize it was pride holding me back and I began to understand it was okay to ask for help. Experiences and self-awareness enhanced my competitive nature. This was a decisive lesson learned in private school.

One last point to make is that failure is something to learn from, rather than fear. My new perspective is you fall, you learn and you continue to push forward. It's not considered a failure if something is learned. You simply change and adjust, because with each fall there is an opportunity to reassess the situation. Figure out what went wrong, why and what preventive measures can be taken to prevent it from happening again. My confidence is to a point that when anyone asks, "what if things don't go right?" the first response is, "what if it goes exactly the way it needs to go?" I understand fear is about attitude.

Unfortunately, the fear of failure stops many people, especially young people, from reaching their full potential, which is one reason I welcome it. It's okay to fall; the key is to get back up, because it's not the end of the world. Seeking counsel and surrounding yourself with people who help build you back up is vital.

Oftentimes fear of failure is typically a worst-case scenario and one literally imagines the absolute worst that could happen. Nine times out of ten, it doesn't get to that point. Try to do what you can and if it doesn't work out, scrap it and try something else. I try to keep moving forward, to keep growing.

The Spiderman Incident

Reading was not my strongest skill growing up and this is where Spiderman enters. My father had a huge collection of superhero comic books he'd saved over the years. By huge I mean thousands of comic books. Love of superheroes was a way to encourage me to work on reading skills.

Pulling out the comic books was our time to sit night after night reading together. There were many superheroes to choose from, but Spiderman was the character I gravitated towards. To this day, Spiderman is my absolute favorite superhero with many people thinking I'm dorky or geeky. However, it's more than superheroes. It's a reminder of where I came from as well as some of the battles and obstacles I've overcome.

As previously identified, during the fourth grade is when I wore my cool, super soft button up Spiderman shirt. I wore it absolutely everywhere, to school, to bed and over to friends. Literally, wear it all the time. My mother had to wait until I fell asleep to remove the shirt in order to wash it, because I refused to take it off.

One day at school, some of the kids sitting in class were saying the shirt was ugly, hated it and were being nasty. During recess, while playing with friends and having a good time, some kids came over and began to physically rip the shirt from my body. Buttons went flying everywhere.

The shirt already had some holes, as it was tattered and old, but this was traumatic because kids were literally shredding the shirt. It was devastating and the one time I went home crying and broken up over an incident. I just couldn't understand why anyone would do this to my favorite shirt.

This was a defining moment and change would come soon.

Perspectives
There are pros and cons to everything in life and the right education environment is no exception. I was not thriving in the public school system, which is why my parents sought another option.

I believe it's not only about education though. It's also about learning to be a person, someone who can actually engage with people and speak to others in complete thoughts. One of the first things the athletic director at the new school taught me is to look people in the eye when you speak to them. Every time we had a conversation, I'd shake the director's hand and look him in the eye. It's funny, because now I look at my generation, as a millennial, and see people struggling to do what I was taught. Many feel uncomfortable.

Not only did I obtain academic knowledge, but learned how vast the world is and the potential opportunities out there. A brand new world opened up. Living in a small home, coming from a low-income environment and going to a local public school gave me a narrow lens to see through. The extent of my existence was going to school and playing video games or basketball or football outside with friends.

Having the opportunity to attend a private school allowed me to experience more of life. I traveled to Europe and saw some cool things. I fell into the Seine River at the Eiffel Tower with my buddies in the middle of February. I now have a clearer understanding of what my job and responsibilities are as a functioning member of society are. I want to try to make it better.

The biggest change from my perspective is I now realize there are no limits to what a person can achieve. Experiences have taught me not to think so small, but to think big.

The perception I had of school changed. Going to private school does cost and paying for tuition along with other expenses is certainly not easy. Though I don't believe it's entirely true, I understand where the stigma comes from that only rich kids go to private school. In Ohio, there are many school choice options. However, Ohio is one of fifty states and more opportunities need to be available throughout the country.

There are options when selecting a college, so there should be alternatives within the K-12 education system. Attending college doesn't have to be an expensive venture due to financial aid and choosing an institution such as community college, which is less expensive and doesn't drastically strain finances. It does require doing research in order to figure out what is the best fit academically and financially. It's important to ensure individuals know what options are available.

I've experienced firsthand the impact education can make on a life and the value it brings. My current perspective is there are no limits to what anyone can achieve and accomplish with a quality education. There is one limiting factor: myself.

Consider Change

When asked what one thing I would change in education, my response is interesting, yet simple. Listen! Listen to parents and students.

Admittedly, this is something most of us are not good at. Typically, when parents reach out to administrators or teachers, often they are not listened to. Parents know their child better than the administrator or teacher, so there needs to be more listening.

One piece of advice I will offer to parents is to be more assertive when communicating with teachers, administrators and others. Establish high expectations, be courageous and persistent, but most of all find the right education environment for your child.

I graduated from high school and am now a college graduate. I have many aspirations, mainly focused on journalism and sports broadcasting. However, I don't want to limit myself to an either/or decision. I've learned to seek opportunity, learned from my failures, realized I have potential and continue to learn skills to help me succeed at whatever I choose to pursue.

The key point is my love of Spiderman gave me an opportunity, which brought awareness and knowledge that I now know my choices are limitless.

My Two Cents

Unfortunately, too many families are not familiar with school choice or aware of the types of alternative education programs legislated in their state. Ohio is a state with several alternatives, yet the programs are not well advertised. Like websites in most states, the Department of Education does not clearly promote alternatives to public school. Therefore, the time and energy involved to ensure families are aware of choices primarily falls on the parents. In addition, the majority of awareness is via word of mouth through friends and/or family members.

Word of mouth isn't the most efficient way to advertise any program. This brings me to the point that there are many forces working against informing parents of school choice options. Fortunately, Walter's family was contacted by a non-profit that is in the business of helping children receive a quality education. After checking into the program, they made the choice, which is what most parents want. Parents want to be given the choice to enroll their child in an education environment more favorable for their child.

From my perspective, fear is the most crippling barrier to success. When we are afraid to step out, get outside our comfort zone, we limit our potential. Making mistakes is part of the learning process and Walter has learned failure is nothing more than an opportunity. Failure should not be a reason or excuse to give up. It is this change in *attitude* that allowed Walter to see failure can drive individuals to realize goals and aspirations and ultimately define success. This is a great lesson to learn and the earlier, the better.

I have to say his Spiderman story is what made me want to learn more about this young man and his education experience. It is unfortunate this story is not unique to other children in the public school system. Too many parents are forced to deal with this type of behavior or worse. Far too often very little to nothing is done to correct bad behavior. There are no consequences and virtually no corrective action is administered. It's no wonder parents are crying out for school choice!

I believe the benefits of a child being in the right education environment far outweigh the hurdles and challenges parents may have to overcome. I am confident most parents want their child to grow up, have useful skills and be productive citizens in society. Therefore, I believe education is the key and foundation for realizing success. It defines how we view life. How choices are made, both good and bad. How we interact with others. How we view ourselves as a person. Most importantly, education shapes how we manage the multitude of challenges life throws at each one of us.

Again, the education environment is critical to developing the attitude a child has as they maneuver their chosen path. Parents must be aware and recognize when an alternative environment is necessary. They must have the courage and resolve to persist in taking the necessary steps to make sure the right fit is found.

I couldn't agree more with the listening component. It is practiced too little. We all want to make sure we are heard, but we are not always willing to hear what others have to say. However, listening is a fundamental component to learning.

Recommendations

Parents – be parents. It is the responsibility of the parent to ensure their child receives a quality education, not the government. Parents need to take ownership of their child's education, help them with their homework, feed, clothe and support them and ensure they have the tools they need to succeed.

If your child is in a failing school, seek information on what education options are in your state. Do not let the public school tell you what they want you to hear. Do your research, make phone calls and connect with non-profits in your state that are advocates for education alternatives.

Get involved in the school Parent Teacher Association (PTA) or Parent Teacher Organization (PTO). Attend meetings, learn the system and advocate for what is best for your child. Share ideas and become the leader that provides creative and innovative programs. There are many individuals and businesses that want to see our children succeed, as they are the future of our communities, states and nation.

The last recommendation I offer to parents is when you believe you are getting the runaround from local officials; contact your state representatives and senators. Ask them for help. They will likely provide information or point you in a direction of someone who is able to provide assistance.

Concluding Notes

The Constitution of Ohio of 1851 with Amendments addresses education in *Article VI, Sections 1-6*. Stemming from the constitution is the Ohio Code where education can be found in Title (33) XXXIII, Chapters 3301-3385.

The Ohio Department of Education (DOE) identifies under *Topics: Ohio's Education Options* the range of education environments offered throughout the state. These include variations for public school, private school, home school, scholarships and more. Because Ohio offers a variety of options, it is critical for parents to understand the education environment their child is immersed in and whether another program might be a good fit.

One non-profit organization, *School Choice Ohio*, focuses on helping families find the right education environment for their child. They reach out to families based on identified criteria to inform parents of the education options offered in Ohio. Their website (scohio.org) states, "School Choice Ohio is committed to helping you find a learning environment that allows your child to grow and thrive."

EdChoice, formerly known as The Friedman Foundation, is a national organization that tracks and provides a range of school choice information and is a good resource for parents.

The organization website (edchoice.org) provides an overview of the five scholarships the state of Ohio offers. The survey data, research and articles EdChoice provides are very helpful to families seeking options.

Lorie

Special Education and Knowing Your Rights | IDEA

Lorie's daughter was born seven weeks premature and diagnosed with cerebral palsy. She developed a bilateral brain hemorrhage while in the intensive care unit. In addition, her premature birth required her to be given a brain shunt immediately.

Our New Norm
Her first two to three years had her in and out of the hospital repeatedly, subsequently needing a second shunt and labeled medically fragile. The seizures began when she was six months old, which led to medication management issues. She is our second child and we were trying to get our bearings. This *new norm* was foreign as our first child was born healthy with no complications.

We wanted to provide as normal a life as we could, which led to our next step of looking into pre-school. We believed this an appropriate option for her. Influencing her learning early would be a benefit to her for peer development, socialization, and overall education.

She remained medically fragile her first twelve years of life and then things settled down. From a developmental standpoint, our daughter is severe and profound in terms of school classification, the label on her Individualized

Education Program (IEP). Her cognition levels identify her expressive skills as non-verbal. We believe her receptive skills are scattered and very high in areas; a child who couldn't sit and color or build blocks. We knew she would always be in a disabilities classroom setting given the degree of brain damage.

Over thirty years later, she's still non-verbal, but uses some signing and gestures. She's incontinent, requires assistance with feeding and full care. She doesn't move around independently. However, this young lady has had tremendous influence in so many people's lives. She's such a blessing, is someone you look at and see the face of God. We know she's been brought to us with purpose.

Attending Public School

Our daughter entered a preschool disabled class at the age of four. She was held back a year due to cognitive delay and entered school age programing at age six. She was center based for three to four years and many problems ensued. The balance of her education was home based through the public school system.

The state of Virginia allows disabled children to remain in public school until the age of twenty-two. We decided to bring her out of the education system at the age of eighteen, because she had maximized school resources to the extent she needed. Our focus shifted to enhancing her learning in a functional home environment and community.

Alternative Education Programs

We were living in Waynesboro, VA at the time. Children with disabilities had very few education options, unless your child was one that needed institutionalization or a clinical placement outside the home. These individuals were operating on a fundamentally different developmental and medical level and were very fragile. When it came to looking for education options, the public school system was pretty much it.

We didn't consider other options. We did not explore private schools to see if they would accept students with disabilities. Retrospectively, I wish we had, but we were young parents in our late twenties with another young child. Everything we went through to get our daughter appropriately educated was traumatic. Our focus was on the serious health issues and trying to understand what education meant for a fragile, disabled child. We were overwhelmed and didn't think beyond public school.

I also think society was struggling with what to do and how to educate children with disabilities in the early 1990s. The struggle was probably more pronounced in the private school setting. I wasn't aware of anyone seeking private school for his or her disabled child, because it's so daunting. Conversely, we also learned peer stimulation and exposure is so important. Based on my general knowledge, I'm not sure private schools have the financial capability or classrooms to educate students with severe disabilities.

We were where we were and made the best decisions with the information we had. The homebound setting was definitely the best for my child.

Primary Factor to Consider
As a parent, it was a tremendous environment to navigate. We spent the first three or four years trying to get our hands around what we'd been dealt. What does it mean? What does the future hold? As a parent you intuitively know you've got

to be the advocate for your child, both educationally and medically. With that comes the weight of suddenly facing circumstances for which you have no frame of reference.

While considering public school we were hopeful and scared, as we didn't know how the public school setting dealt with individuals with disabilities. We didn't know if she could receive what we felt was an appropriate level of care, curriculum and intervention.

When I first went into school meetings, I would find myself using the word *optimal,* in that I wanted an optimal education setting. The more informed I became through researching regulations and increasing my knowledge of the system, I discovered the right word was *appropriate.* This is a legal perspective, but the right expectation for parents to have because schools are not going to be taxed with legally giving an optimal setting. It doesn't work that way! We geared our expectations to where we were confident she was in a safe, secure and prosperous environment to maximize her skill sets.

We were under no illusion she would *grow out of this*; it is a lifetime diagnosis. Early on we decided to do everything we could to help maximize her capacity to learn, socialize and be part of the community. We didn't set expectations such as read by the time she was in the 5th grade or be delayed and read by 8th grade. If that's her capacity, great! We'll get there with the right curriculum, teachers and interventions, which will be revealed over time.

We went into the public education system apprehensive and frightened, understanding we had much to learn.

Hurdles Encountered

To some extent, the worries a parent has are relative. If you don't have a child with disabilities, you still worry about your child's learning environment, teacher quality, interactions and relationships. Having a child with disabilities sets the bar higher. I had to come to grips with the fact I was going to drop her off somewhere for the day. I would go to the parking lot, get in my car and leave a child who couldn't speak, tell me how her day was, tell me if anybody was mistreating her, or God forbid, abusing her in some way. I had to place a level of trust in strangers, which scared me to death, but you have to employ trust.

I went through a period where I sat in for an hour or so and observed. One of the biggest hurdles was the limited number of K-12 disabled students. There were not the resources or the desire to create age appropriate disability classrooms. Students in K through 5 or 6 were put in multiple disability classes. This placed our medically fragile kindergarten child with cognition issues in a class with 5th and 6th graders, some three times her size.

There was a teacher and aide, which may have met regulations, yet the reality of supervision and actual learning was challenging. As with any classroom, children are learning at various paces and requiring different supports and resources. Disability classrooms need to be broken down even further. Understanding functional learning is different with each student and requires an IEP. Some students have dual diagnosis, which can include deficits in physical movement and speech.

She was the youngest in her first classroom and there were no resources for her. There were no age appropriate developmental toys and no curriculum. My classroom observations quickly revealed my child was left sitting for the time she *needed to be there* with no interventions and no resources.

As a parent of a disabled child, I became aware of an innate being within myself I never knew was there. It was a strong advocate that said this is not good enough, not appropriate and I've got to do something about it.

The IEP was my first pursuit, which was totally foreign in terms of my role and what it means. I identified resources to help me understand this maze and actually figured out my daughter has rights.

Nobody told me that on the school side because that works against them. Once I learned this, I was a beast with three heads to a school administrator. This is unfortunate, because it should be a team approach and what is best for the student. After all, we know our child best. We discovered parents are legally entitled to be part of the team.

I quickly learned the IEP process along with understanding rights and special education regulations. The first thing I advocated for was to provide my daughter with a student aide. Not a classroom aide, but a dedicated aide. This is someone who will be with her for the time she's in the classroom. The schools fought me for quite some time, because it's all about money. This is an expenditure dedicated solely to one student.

My advocacy, and frankly the difficult person I had to become to get things done, resulted in creating another disabilities classroom in another elementary school. This segmented the younger population from the older population, which was definitely a step in the right direction. Eventually my daughter was placed in a more appropriate learning environment with a student aide. By this time I was informed and had figured out how to work the system, which is unfortunately what we have to do.

Her health continued to be a problem in the school setting. Every time she had the onset of an illness, she would have a predicating seizure. Once her seizures were under control, she developed a severe latex allergy. It became apparent during one of her birthdays when she had an anaphylactic reaction to latex balloons and could not breath adequately. After that occurrence, she was officially diagnosed.

Most days I would get called thirty minutes after school started to pick her up. Apparently there was latex somewhere in the classroom causing allergic reactions. Removing her from the classroom greatly improved her breathing. This posed a serious liability situation for the schools. They did the right thing and took the classroom apart bolt by bolt to try to figure out latex sources. The foundation was declared idiopathic, meaning no source was found.

The only thing we could default to was something in the ventilation system. We also considered the fact, like all students, she was in a classroom setting where people carry germs and get sick. Based on these issues, I pursued homebound education, which was a fight never to be forgotten.

During the latex situation, I was provided homebound temporarily. I had to get documentation restating my daughter's baseline, both medically and educationally. I had to obtain special, independent evaluations from the University of Virginia to validate my daughter's least restrictive environment (LRE). This is a critical term to understand. It simply means students should be placed in an environment that is not inappropriately or overly restrictive to peers, socialization, access, etc. My daughter's LRE was ultimately at home, which promoted good health and enabled her to learn in a qualitative manner.

Education has evolved into what is called mainstreaming, a term used to integrate students with disabilities into classrooms with peers, as appropriate. It is recognized as the LRE in many cases. Many school districts have gone to nothing but mainstream classrooms with no self-contained disability classrooms. I don't subscribe to this concept. Some children need to learn in an isolated setting. However, they should have exposure to their peers. They are legally entitled to that through federal legislation, the Individuals with Disabilities Education Act.

My daughter became homebound and was provided physical therapy (PT), occupational therapy (OT) and speech, which I had to continue to fight for to ensure her needs were met. It became necessary to retain an attorney because her IEP was not being followed in the classroom or home based environment. We were not believed or could be relied upon.

IEP meetings have staff sitting on one side of the table and parents on the other, which sets a sense of us vs. them. Regardless, our attorney helped us convey we were serious about our daughter's welfare, even in the public school setting. We wanted to ensure she would get what she was legally entitled to, which did lead to a very intense and adversarial experience.

The school would never admit her shortcomings or their failure to legally comply with the law. However, the situation improved with a new teacher and, more importantly, a *team* effort with a mom who was willing to do whatever it took. I often wonder and worry about children who do not have informed and engaged parents. Most parents desire to be part of their child's education experience, but the system is not set up that way.

In the end, being in a homebound program allowed her health to improve dramatically. Seizures were under control and she was actually learning and achieving some benchmark milestones. It became clear early on that home was her LRE, but through the public school setting.

Taking on Public Policy

The experiences and difficulties with the school system were rooted in the decisions and lack of regard for children with disabilities demonstrated by the Director of Student Services, in my opinion. From my perspective, the administrator did not have insight for what the needs were, nor cared.

Other than advocate for my daughter, I decided the best way to affect change was to try to influence public policy by running for public office. My focus was to influence the regulatory approach to public schools, with specific attention to children with disabilities and I did have opportunities to influence policy.

I was able to influence how classrooms were set up and the role parents should play in the school setting. I was successful in setting up a special education advisory council to the school board. The council was comprised of parents and specialists who advised the school board on matters pertaining to K-12 special education. I was able to place parental representation on the budget review teams, which gave parents a voice in allocation of resources and in the advocacy of children with disabilities. These initiatives gave me great pride.

In my role as a parent and school board member, I learned I had to fundamentally break things down educationally to a finite level in order to teach children with disabilities. We know intuitively when teaching general education that the foundation needs to be there for all students. It needs to be there early and curriculum needs to grow accordingly.

Regarding disabilities, I served on a disabilities council that reported to the City Council. I was able to work across domains while on the school board through the Virginia School Board Association (VSBA), though my platform there was much broader than just disabilities. All the experiences and knowledge I gained personally and professionally enabled me to not only serve those with disabilities, but the population at-large.

Three of my four years on the school board, I was fortunate to be Chair. It was through this term I intuitively knew I had found *my lane*. I was seeking to have a broader influence platform of experience, so I ran for City Council against a popular incumbent and won.

The parent of a special needs child understands how to break down fundamental learning to a level where the child can learn. I knew intuitively as an elected official, especially on the school board, fundamental early childhood education is imperative. When I talk about platforms of influence, it means having a voice to serve people and entities in an informed manner. This hopefully results in new and improved mandates.

I had so many opportunities while serving in elected office. I became a known resource for parents who needed help navigating IEP's and the world of special education. Overall, I've been very blessed with opportunities to serve and help many families.

Obstacle to Overcome

It was appropriate classroom settings and fighting for rights. It's unfortunate I have to say this, but the reality is the majority of schools do not benefit by letting parents know their child's rights. It is common for parents to be given a summarized handout in small print outlining rights. That's why it's so important for parents of disabled children to arm themselves with information and knowledge about all of the regulations and rights.

Fighting for rights as well as fighting to get an appropriate classroom setting were the two biggest obstacles.

Government Regulation

One of the most significant regulations for special education is the IEP, a legal compliance document. Once executed, it's legally binding. If something is not in an IEP, the schools are not required to provide. The smallest of things should be included, such as having a test read to your child. When I speak about regulations, I'm referring to IEP compliance and noncompliance.

Time is spent creating the document and when schools don't follow through with it, I wonder what's the point of having the IEP. The benefit is to have a legal document with punitive action attached to it, which parents have the right to pursue, but they need to know they have the right. This is where parental and student rights come into play.

Special education regulations are lengthy and complex. For example, Section 504 legislation prohibits discrimination for persons with disabilities in programs that receive federal funding. The federal legislation titled Individuals with Disabilities Education Act (IDEA) intimidates most parents. It's sad we have to tell parents to read the legislation to know their rights. Initially, parents are overwhelmed and don't know where to look. Parents aren't thrilled about sitting and reading regulations, but the minute there's a problem, that's the first place to try to find a defense to solve the problem.

Special education is riddled with regulations and I believe the primary purpose of regulations should be to protect the student. In some cases, regulations are written too broadly and give schools too much latitude and protection. It has been years since I've looked at them, but regulations do change and it requires parents to keep up with the changes.

Learning the multiple levels of bureaucracy on the fly is the last thing parents want to think about when they have a child with disabilities. However, parents must understand their involvement is essential. My experience was heavy involvement, but I will say a high percentage of parents do not get involved. They trust the schools to do what's right or feel overwhelmed based on frustration and ambivalence.

Parents should be able to yield to the schools as a best practice, but reality tells us different. You see the difference in the children. It's very apparent and it's sad to see children with disabilities who are not cultivated and cared for at home. Sometimes school is their *soft place to fall.*

IDEA is the primary federal regulation for disabled children and public education. However, Virginia is a Dillon's Rule state, which means localities can adopt regulations locally. In theory, states have some flexibility as long as they remain within the perimeters of state legislation. Nonetheless, state Departments of Education implement and manage based on federal and state law.

A Few Experiences

I remember an experience in my daughter's classroom where it ran the gambit of disabilities and ages. I walked in for an observation and there was a male and female, both older disabled children, on top of each other with no supervision. This was a turning point for me and I quickly understood blaming the teacher was not totally appropriate. Teachers don't have the resources needed given the span of ages and disabilities. Putting these children in one classroom with one teacher and one aide was unrealistic. I'm talking about lunchtime, snack time and diaper changing, because these are not typical classrooms. This was a very pivotal moment when I started thinking about inadequacy in terms of resources.

Another incident is when my daughter was in a more appropriate classroom that actually had a bathroom in it. The teacher was very rigorous for a special education teacher; meaning squares went into square holes and nothing else. I brought my daughter home from school one evening and she wouldn't let me change her diaper. She was fearful and it became obvious something was not right.

The next day it got worse. I called our pediatrician, who actually came to the house and I had to inquire as to whether something had happened to my daughter or if she had been violated. The doctor did an examination and thanks to the good Lord above, she had not been violated. However, she continued to have negative behavior when changing her diaper. I voiced my concerns to the school and they conducted what was said to be an *investigation*. Unfortunately, there was no investigation and no finding, which is what I expected, as they weren't going to assume any responsibility.

What I learned through classroom observations is the bathroom is small and narrow. Knowing the teacher's vigorous approach, I quickly learned she was taking my daughter into the bathroom, closing the door and this was scaring my daughter. She has vestibular issues, which means when you force her to lie down, she panics. Today this would be a form of abuse.

This was serious because my daughter should not have to endure an environment that caused this level of trauma to change her diaper. Retrospectively, I had to say to myself:

1. What should have been done?
2. What kind of bathroom should have been in the classroom?
3. Where should my child have been changed?
4. Why did the teacher keep doing this when it was quite apparent my child was traumatized by it?

These two examples were polarizing and upsetting as a parent and I questioned what I would do with the information. I was dealing with a school system that was fighting me at every turn. I knew my daughter was traumatized, but with no substantive investigative finding, I thought I had nowhere to turn.

Life After Public School

Things progressed and I pulled my daughter out of public school education when she reached the legal age of eighteen. We obtained guardianship, as she will never be independent or completely able to care for herself. She was plateauing through her homebound experiences and the teachers weren't seeing much progression. Her functionality in the home was greater then what the schools and resource therapies were providing. We decided to switch direction and work on maximizing functional skills.

She needed help developing appropriate functional skills with eating, navigating her environment, and those kinds of things. She'll never be a vocational learner. Her cognition wouldn't allow for participation in a sheltered workshop setting. So, we took steps to have her more integrated with family, neighbors and peers and let her home be a functional place of success. We focused on having her in the most optimal environment for her happiness and welfare. As she grew and had opportunities to do different things, she progressed.

We found success in fundamental things, even though we wanted our child to be able to do all the things normal children do. It's a sobering reality when you're the parent of a disabled child at the level our daughter will always be. You've got to turn the corner at some point in your thinking. We are blessed and believe this child was given to us for a reason. We'll provide the best for her and do our best to provide resources, while ensuring her exposure to community is everything it can and should be.

At the end of the day we want to look back and say we did it right. We don't have any regrets. We left no stone unturned where her care is concerned. We did the best to ensure a safe and successful education environment, though it was a challenging environment and don't ever want to do it again. I'm sure I would still be the mother with three heads and probably worse, because I've been through it once.

Now that our daughter is older, my role is to continue supporting her needs and loving her. As a bonus, I continue to help families who have disabled family members. I have a different perspective based on my experience. My child's cold is a much more serious issue, but it's all relative.

There's such an appreciation you derive from being the parent of a disabled child and coming up through a public education environment. The exposure is holistically good, but you've got to know how to do it. You must learn, but if you choose not to, make an informed decision to trust the schools to do the best they can. That's not a bad thing. However, if you want to ensure the wellbeing of knowing your child's needs are being met in a school environment, your advocacy is essential.

Benefit of Your Decision
A positive for my daughter was being in mainstream classrooms with her peers before we pulled her from center-based learning for health reasons. Another positive is she wasn't at home all the time. This enabled her to be in another setting and the opportunity to be in a different environment.

This may sound a bit weird, but experiencing some of the challenges we faced to advocate on her behalf, I now acknowledge as a positive. In some sense we believe we carved the way to help other families. In some ways things may have been going on all along for other families, but they didn't know how to deal with it. That is a positive, which comes from the many learned experiences. I would never want to go through this again, but the positives are there.

When you have a child with disabilities, you are overwrought with burden and guilt as a parent. You feel you could have done something different to realize a better outcome. For example, the guilt of wondering what I may have done that made me go into labor early. I don't want to say it's all necessarily negative. It's dealing with the reality of the situation.

I think my daughter enjoyed going to school to some extent, once she was put in an appropriate classroom. There were some pretty cool things for her to play with and learn from. She experienced a well-equipped physical therapy room, which evolved over time due to parent involvement. There was a handicapped swing on the playground, which allowed her to enjoy recreation with her peers. There was access to things she normally would not have had in a home setting and these were positives. She did struggle with parental separation when left at school, like many young children.

My sister-in-law, who teaches disabled individuals, has helped me realize things have changed and improved in today's public education environment. For some of us who were around in the early 90s, maybe we were influential in helping shine the light on defining appropriate classrooms and resources. My daughter was in school when the standards of learning (SOL) were introduced followed by No Child Left Behind (NCLB), which was the foundation for analyzing students in categorized populations. This was a curve ball with respect to how schools faired with testing results and accreditation. Again, a lot to learn!

There are pros and cons. Our experiences were certainly challenging and negative at times. Leaving my child in a school environment I feared was something I will never forget. The bar is high for parents of disabled children, but the silver lining is I learned so much. My daughter got what she needed and the ability to help other families cannot be overstated. Our children are so worth it! They are angels that walk among us, untouched by the negatives in our world.

I Would Like to Change ....

Generally, everything comes down to money when talking about education. My experience on the school board re-enforced this in my mind. As I think and dream about an *optimal* education experience for students with disabilities, it comes down to resources, tangible and intangible, that are *mandated* for our children. There aren't resources without money.

I'm mindful of the demand for quality teachers and staff. They are individuals *called* to this profession and are extensions of our families. I would like to see education budgeting held harmless from cuts and, in fact, increased year to year.

Serving at the local level enabled me to look at students and evaluate needs. I was successful in working with our city council to set a funding formula for school revenue. In Virginia, school boards do not have taxing authority and this promotes an adversarial relationship between the two bodies. That was not good enough for me, so we worked very hard to successfully cultivate a relationship with our city council, based on trust and respect.

As I reflect back on my son's education experiences, so much has changed. He is a product of public schools and has grown into a fine young man with a wonderful education foundation. Public school was the right environment for him. There were not many choices available for my daughter, whose needs required a very tailored approach. But guess what, she was legally entitled to it.

In a best-case scenario, I would like diverse resources available for different levels of learning. The best and brightest teachers paid what they should be paid as well as a healthy learning environment. Too many schools in our country are antiquated, old with unhealthy environments and not structured for 21st century learning. Schools need appropriate resources to ensure each and every student, including those with disabilities, have the opportunity to maximize their potential.

Children are the product of their learning environment. We all carry a tremendous burden whether working to support a family, an elected official or a teacher, whatever your circumstance. As adults, it is our responsibility to ask if we're doing the best for our children. To ensure education experiences are enabling them to enter adulthood to be productive members of society. This is a tall order to fill and we're not going to catch every child, but we have the responsibility to put the structure in place where we make an attempt to capture every child.

Another priority is for students to learn at the appropriate level to maximize their potential. One shoe does not fit all. Let's aspire to a variety of resources and curriculum for functionality. We need to consider career and technical education as well as college bound students. Some children simply need functionality. Special education or Asperger's children that function on high levels, they need an education structured for them to be successful in their world. I'd like to see broader thinking about what we're doing with our children, wherever they're being educated.

Education choices are imperative, because not all children can learn in a public school setting. Parents need to decide, whatever the choice may be and thank goodness there are choices. Parents need to understand it is a *choice* and should be looked at carefully to make sure their child is getting the best education.

Closing Thoughts

One thing I would say is we need to do a better job of having a continuum of placement out of the home. When disabled children come out of the public education system and not functionally able to work or go to college, there is a need for transitional placement. We need to consider settings outside of the home environment such as day programs that provide peer stimulation and functional learning opportunities.

I was pursuing options where we previously lived and looked at things like sheltered workshops and day programs, but unfortunately were not options for my daughter. Where we currently live, there are no day programs other than what is an hour away and not realistic for us. Once children get out of the school system, they're in society, the real world. Society has a higher burden when looking at individuals with disabilities. It's not okay to say they've come through school, now they can sit at home.

Not all individuals with disabilities as adults have family structure. They become victim to a foster care type system. There are not enough conversations legislatively about what we can do. As members of our communities, we can enrich our lives through giving of time, talent and resources to those in need. Inclusion and respect go a long way. I'm proud to say I have witnessed an evolution of inclusion and respect for those with disabilities in my lifetime.

As we've evolved over time with our daughter, we have lived through different phases, with different challenges. Being the *mom with three heads* is not something I would have ever imagined, but the situation demanded a strong advocacy approach. As parents, we do what we need to do for our children, with no apologies.

The world of disabilities is a difficult subject and has always been somewhat polarizing. Those who have historically been judgmental were of that mindset largely due to a lack of understanding and we've come a long way as a society. Public school has been instrumental in forcing the conversation of integration due to mainstreaming requirements.

When we're in restaurants with our daughter, you quickly realize she's not able to talk, is sometimes boisterous and has certain behaviors. People now embrace her and us and go so far as to help. Twenty years ago, people would have been starring and giving *oh my goodness* looks. Now it's a different environment, generally and socially.

I would be remiss if I didn't mention the loving and caring father my daughter has. We have been married over thirty-seven years and though *I* is used often in this story, the journey is about what *we* have done. It is nothing short of extraordinary. Statistically, most couples do not make it when they have a disabled child. My husband has been my rock and his little girl's prince. To this day, the care he renders is one hundred percent reflective of the level of care I provide as mom. He recently retired and significantly shares in our daughter's care. We are truly blessed!

Our daughter drove me to run for elected office. I knew there was a need to address policy based on the insights I realized in terms of whose fighting for these children. Also, it was important to help parents connect the dots. The convictions I felt led me to perform over thirty years of non-profit/public service work. Credit must be given to our daughter and what she has taught me.

In closing, I strongly encourage parents to reach out and become informed. Be part of your child's education experience. There will be moments during your child's development that may look like baby steps, but are truly stepping-stones moving them to the next level of learning. Celebrate your child's abilities!

What I Think:

As a former sitting public school board member, I wonder what has really changed. My experience is more current and I'm viewing from a different perspective. When I began my term on the school board, the district was awaiting the results of a state investigation regarding IEPs and other issues dealing with special needs children. Parents were advocating for their children, but to no avail. Not until they banded together and involved their state senator did any action take place. The result was the state did an investigation, filed a report and provided some training and process recommendations. Personnel changes were made and life continues. However, are things better?

I'm not convinced there were any substantive changes made. But one thing is certain; as long as parents stay quiet, you can guarantee nothing will change.

Over the past several years, I've had opportunities to talk with parents of children with special needs and listened to the difficulties they've encountered. Many parents speak about the IEP, mainly how it's not followed. Some battle with scheduling meetings to discuss behavior issues and trying to ensure they can reach a workable solution. Others struggle with trying to ensure their child is safe from being bullied in the learning environment. One thing is a given, too many parents get tired of fighting the system.

I have come to believe children with disabilities are far too often dismissed, ignored or simply overlooked in some education settings. Most school systems hire special education teachers where the demands and expectations are exponential. Teachers are required to obtain a degree, but college programs tend to be antiquated based on an antiquated model and often do not provide sufficient applicable, practical hands-on opportunities.

There are always exceptions to everything, but having a teaching degree and license does not automatically make a good teacher. In addition, there are required endorsements based on the position. Special education teachers must obtain an endorsement, which requires additional credit hours sanctioned by the state. Becoming a teacher requires dedication and commitment. However, the majority of higher learning institutions offer education programs as a minor, which in my mind is an indicator as to the level of importance placed on the profession.

Like Lorie, my experience leads me to the same conclusion that disparities are related to funding. Many school systems are ill equipped to handle and provide the necessary resources, whether it be qualified teachers, teaching supports and tools or ensuring there is an appropriate learning environment. However, I am not in favor of school boards having funding authority.

Speaking of funding, children who have IEPs are a funding source for the public school system. According to the National Center for Education Statistics (NCES) the number of children between the ages of three to twenty-one continues to rise. NCES states in 2017-2018, there were seven million public school students receiving special education services, while thirty-four percent had specific learning disabilities. If only thirty-four percent of students have specific disabilities, then what qualifies the remaining sixty-six percent for services? I surmise this includes children who are bored with sitting in a classroom who are labeled inattentive, hyperactive or ADHD.

I will reiterate the best advocate for any child is the parent. When it comes to expectations, parents need to make sure they are clear about what they are legally afforded for their disabled child. If an IEP is not being followed, the parent needs to make it known and, if necessary, be the *three-headed beast* in order to ensure their child is in the appropriate learning environment.

I've seen too many parents become frustrated, demoralized and even bullied when it comes to being their child's advocate. I admit it is difficult to fight a bureaucracy and education is a big, bureaucratic system. However, parents need to stand up for what is legal, appropriate and right, because that is their job. Don't surrender parental authority to the system. Stand firm and the optimist in me believes the parent can overcome. Remember: there is strength in numbers!

Recommendations:

I would encourage parents to seek out various sources to become an informed advocate. Do not take the word of any one individual, do the research, ask questions and know the law. Yes, IDEA and 504 legislation and state statutes are boring and can be intimidating, but the old saying is true: *knowledge is power*. To ensure your child is receiving the appropriate tools to be as successful as they can possibly be, it is incumbent upon the parent to be their voice. Don't sit back and trust the system. Parents can trust, but they must verify. The system depends on the ignorance of parents knowing their rights.

There is a wide range of non-profits in states and throughout the nation skilled in helping parents advocate for their special needs child. Do an Internet search and don't hesitate to contact any that may be able to help. I've found that most organizations are willing to share and help in any way they can. If they are not able to provide direct assistance, they most likely will be able to direct you to an organization that can.

Contact your elected local and state officials to see what they are able to provide. They receive phone calls and letters asking for assistance on a multitude of issues and this includes dealing with the education system. At the least, they should be able to help with identifying potential resources and organizations.

There are many avenues to explore when dealing with the education system to ensure children with disabilities is provided appropriate accommodations. Parents might want to consider using a mediator or lawyer to help them navigate the process, ending in a result they are comfortable with. Word of caution: there are financial expectations to this choice and there are no guaranteed results.

Concluding Notes:

The Individuals with Disabilities Education Act (IDEA) is federal law and all states must comply with the regulatory elements. Parents can find the statutes and regulations on the United States Department of Education website (www.ed.gov). You will find the link to the IDEA page under "Laws & Guidance."

As with every state, the state constitution includes an article and sections regarding education. The Virginia Constitution includes Article VIII: Education, Sections 1-11, which speaks to roles and responsibilities. Title 22.1 in the Code of Virginia identifies applicable statutes.

Care.com posted an article in June 2017 that identifies ten special needs organizations, which provide a range of supports for various disabilities and ages. The list can be found at https://www.care.com/c/stories/6620/10-helpful-special-needs-organizations/

Kelley

Sentenced by the System

Kelley, a divorced single mother, found herself in jail for registering her two daughters in the school district where her parents lived. Like many struggling parents, this is not uncommon. This act of enrolling her daughters in the school district where her parents lived changed their lives in ways many Americans couldn't possibly conceive.

A question Kelley's story conjures up is *how can this happen in America?* The greatest nation on earth! Sending a mother to jail because she wants a better education for her children can't possibly happen. America is not communist Russia or theocratic Iran. We don't live in a police state.

This story seems extreme and inconceivable. Like millions of parents, Kelley knew her daughters were receiving a sub-par education because of their zip code. Registering children in school districts where a brother, sister, grandparent or relative lives happens every year. Kelley merely sought quality education and help with before and after school care.

Public Education Districts

We lived in the Akron, Ohio school district. Our inner-city environment concerned me, particularly when it came to the local public schools my daughters were attending.

Going through a divorce, I welcomed the help my parents were able to provide. Not only was I a single mother working full-time, but working on furthering my education. Life was difficult; finances were limited and trying to do my best to stay afloat. Having moved to Akron, we became aware the school district had academic and behavior challenges. One daughter was in elementary and the other going into Junior High School. I was particularly concerned and nervous about the school my oldest daughter would be attending.

Based on the current situation, I knew I needed help. My parents lived in the Copley-Fairlawn school district, west of Akron. The schools were rated good academically and had less behavior issues than schools in the Akron district. With my daughters attending schools in the Copley-Fairlawn district, this would solve the need with before and after school care.

This is when my father suggested they could help. This offer of support led me to enroll them in the Copley-Fairlawn school district for the 2007/2008 academic years.

Copley-Fairlawn School District

The first year everything was fine and the schools were superb. My daughters were doing well, were spending time with their grandparents and life was good. The second year things changed. I received a notification from the school district informing me an investigator was hired to determine our place of residence. Honestly, I was surprised to learn people were hired to perform these services.

Once notification was received, my father and I took steps to get a grandparent power of attorney so they would be legally enrolled. The legal document was provided to the school, but the district stated they wanted them dis-enrolled.

The 2008/2009 school years had already begun and wanted my daughters to complete the year, but the district decided to pursue legal action as the remedy. A hearing was held where the judge ruled in favor of them finishing the school year. Based on the ruling, I left my daughters in the Copley-Fairlawn district.

The school district chose to fight the legal decision over the winter months. In June of the second year, I received a letter from the judge informing me that I needed to remove my daughters from the schools, which I complied with.

My philosophy is *life goes on* and they were removed. Thinking this ended the matter, approximately eighteen months later my father and I received indictment letters. The district subsequently filed charges of fraud and record tampering based on the address identified on the enrollment forms. The district claimed this to be a false statement.

This was a complete shock to the family. I've done my best to live right, have never broken the law or been in trouble. Maybe a parking ticket, but never anything considered really bad. My primary concern, though, was my father and couldn't believe I had involved him in this situation. A large part of my concern was due to his poor health.

I ended up standing trial, was found guilty and sentenced to ten days in jail, with three years probation to include monthly check-ins with a parole officer. Also, I was required to do forty hours of counseling, eighty hours of community service and pay some financial costs.

More to the Story

Though my father and I were both charged and stood trial together, the court found him not guilty. He did not enroll his granddaughters and the address was legally his.

Yet, this was not the end. An investigation began into my father's social security and disability benefits. I'm not exactly sure what the issue was, other than there seemed to be some confusion regarding social security and Medicare, but theft charges were brought against my father. I remember the press writing horrible articles saying he stole a crazy amount of money, something like one hundred thousand dollars, for healthcare or health insurance. We were baffled; none of us were lawyers and didn't fully understand what was going on. The family was scared and knew we couldn't fight this. It was too massive for us to comprehend.

During the jury selection phase, we were waiting to be called into the courtroom. We walked in, sat down and the Prosecutor looked at us and stated, "Justice is just like beauty; it's in the eye of the beholder." We thought this is not a good sign. The impression this statement left is, this is meant to be a message to the community and we're going to be the example.

My father was sentenced to one-year in the penitentiary and entered the facility in May. By July, he told the family he was not able to walk. He had been diagnosed with *clostridia*, a bacterium that causes trauma sufficient to interrupt the blood supply to large muscle groups. By winter, he was on dialysis with a trachea in his throat. Sadly, he did not survive his one-year sentence.

On top of this, a journalist from the Akron Beacon Journal continued to write negative, disparaging articles. The journalist had grown up in the Copley area; his children attended the schools and had developed long-standing relationships. My family believed the district would call and he would write the most horrific articles, which took a toll on the family.

Education Options

At the time I decided to enroll my daughters in the Copley-Fairlawn school district, I was not aware of alternative education programs. I knew there were private schools, but believed this was not a realistic option given our financial situation.

During the period of time in the Copley-Fairlawn district, a friend informed me of the Ohio EdChoice program. Though this program was not well advertised, I did look into the program during the eighteen months of our ordeal. I made contact with EdChoice and was informed my youngest daughter was eligible for enrollment in a private school.

The public schools don't tell you or let you know this is what is available and this is what's offered. Parents find out about alternative education programs only via word of mouth. Public schools were not providing information or sharing what options were available to parents.

Two Daughters – Two School Environments

Both daughters returned to their locally assigned school district in Akron. As previously stated, the younger daughter was offered a scholarship under the EdChoice program and enrolled in the Emmanuel Christian Academy, a private school close to their Akron address. The private school was better; there were fewer behavior issues, no bullying, smaller classrooms and teachers seemed more in-tune with child needs. Bullying is one of the biggest things I absolutely can't stand and this was a good fit for my younger daughter.

The older daughter was entering high school and not eligible for the EdChoice program, at that time. Employed at the local public high school where my daughter would be attending, I was familiar with the school. It was known for being an aggressive inner city school where a high number of parents provided foster care or were incarcerated. The academics were not the best and safety was a major concern.

My oldest daughter shared with me that the new school was very different. The transition was a very difficult adjustment. I remember her telling me students took about thirty to thirty-five minutes to settle down, but the class period is only fifty minutes. Students would sit on desks, throw things, tease and pick on each other. Many will say *kids will be kids*, but they can also be very mean at times. There were several little things she was trying to cope with, but I knew this was not the education environment I wanted for her.

Hurdles to Overcome
The family struggled through this life-changing ordeal in many ways and over several years, which included mental and physical health challenges. It is an understatement to say this was a horrific ordeal, to be convicted of felony charges and the press continuing to follow and write about the story. I believe the penal system was as unforgiving as the education system.

With the education system against me, the judicial system fighting me, the press continuing to write negative articles to keep the story in the news, it's no wonder I went through one of the deepest depressions ever imagined. Branded an *undesirable* in my community, struggling to stay afloat, raising my daughters and trying to make sense of this whole ordeal, I did think my life was completely over.

But, the primary hurdle is the day the judge announced the sentence. I remember the judge looking me in the eye and saying something along the lines of, she would do what she could to make sure I never work or never get my license or never teach again. This was a significant mental jolt, because I worked in the public education system at the time. My passion was to help students with their many needs and to support struggling children.

The irony of the judge's statement is not lost. I continue to work in a classroom with students who have behavior issues. I help students in my community get the most from an education environment many feel trapped in.

A ray of sunshine appeared when Ohio Governor John Kasich intervened. The case was reviewed and the decision made to reduce the charges and eliminate the felonies. This act by the Governor provided hope with a much-needed element of comfort. This act has allowed me to integrate back into society with no criminal record.

The saying *when given lemons, make lemonade* is true in this case. Though there were many dark days, I was not alone. My belief that God is using me for good has opened up opportunities to speak and teach in ways I never could comprehend prior to this experience. In addition, my knowledge of the education system is greatly expanded, which has provided a new set of lenses to look through at the world.

My current focus is not only on helping children, but also sharing my story with parents, grandparents and others. My ability to speak and share this ordeal is a type of therapy. I believe it is also therapeutic for those I speak with because they know they're not alone in their fight, whatever their fight may be.

Life Continues

Over nine years has passed since our family experienced this dark period. Yet life does continue regardless of what happens along the journey. This ordeal has given me a platform to speak and to support various causes. I'm an advocate for school choice and believe I can advocate for choice in other arenas, because choice is part of daily decision-making.

This platform affords opportunities to share and address issues I'm passionate about. I was invited to share part of my story at a national education conference. Was seated in the audience when two cases affecting choice were argued at the U.S. Supreme Court. The first case was Friedrichs v. California Teachers Association (CTA). The second case was Janus v. American Federation of State, County and Municipal Employees (AFSCME). Both cases involved labor union practices, which are choice issues as well.

I've appeared on talk shows and was featured in a couple of documentaries. One experience is rather humorous. The John Stossel Show contacted me when he was with Fox News. After accepting the invitation and agreeing to fly to New York City for the interview, a few family members and friends shared they were aghast. The general sentiment was I shouldn't go because it's Fox News and once I entered the studio, I'd never return. Well, I did return to Ohio and shared that John Stossel is one of the most humble, nicest gentlemen I've ever met.

Yes, time has passed, but the emotional and mental scars are ever present. I still tear up and my voice does crack when I begin to speak about the ordeal. Particularly about my father's involvement and his subsequent case. I admit there are some things even time cannot heal. However, I do have a goal, which is to get through a speaking engagement without letting my emotions take over.

My Two Cents:

Let me step back and share that I first heard a snippet of Kelley's story at an education conference in Nashville, TN in Nov 2017. She was one of several panelists who shared an abbreviated rendition of their individual experiences with the public education system in their respective states. Each story was interesting, thought provoking, and moving, but I have to admit I was literally *shocked* when I heard this story.

The response I personally had led me to seek her out in order to hear the rest of the story. I also had a desire to try to understand how this could happen. From my perspective she was merely seeking an education environment where her daughters would receive quality academics, not be bullied, picked on and have an element of safety.

Hearing her speak, researching news articles and interviewing her, I can understand how she views this as a tragedy and a blessing. It was an extremely difficult time when she was in the middle of the storm, but looking back she sees the blessings of weathering the storm. Once a storm has passed, we are able to grasp that hindsight is 20/20.

The pain of losing her father will always linger and that will never change. On the other hand, the knowledge and experience she now has helps bring hope to so many others. This is because of the journey she traveled.

With that said, I still ponder the reasons why this happened. It is true she enrolled her daughters in the public school district her parents lived in. It is true the public schools in her district could only offer low performing schools with unsafe environments, like so many inner city schools.

To me this experience of enrolling her daughters in the Copley-Fairlawn school district in Ohio is utterly and totally mindboggling. Parents want their children to receive a quality education and enrolling out of district close to family members is a common practice. In fact, all around the country every year parents enroll children in school districts that are not their zip code assigned school. Even the Copley-Fairlawn district confirmed there were other children enrolled illegally.

So, we must contemplate, "does it rise to the level where the school district hires a private investigator and shoots video of Kelley driving her daughters to school?" as ABC News reported. Are her actions worthy of seeking a legal solution, which resulted in felony charges? Personally, I do not believe this should happen and though I don't know all the facts, my experience of sitting on a public school board leads me to speculate there were more realistic remedies that should have been pursued.

I view this as a very extreme case and more than likely contribute the actions taken around a lack of and/or breakdown in communication. For whatever reason, my perception is it appears the district was not willing to engage in a practical discussion that would result in a sensible solution. They were unprofessional, not inclined to provide information or take reasonable steps to resolve the situation amicably and chose to pursue an adversarial legal solution.

As reported by Ebony, the result is Kelley faced felony charges, spent time in jail, on probation and performing community service. Her father faced felony charges, was sent to prison, lost his home and died in prison in 2012. These pursuits radically changed one life and ended another.

Who do we believe? This may appear to be a "he said, she said" scenario. Did the school district reach out to Kelley and her father to propose a remedy? In 2011 NPR interviewed the superintendent of the Copley-Fairlawn school district and stated the administration worked very hard and tried to work through the issues. However, Kelley complied with the court order, handed down in the second year, and the daughters were removed at the end of the school year.

The superintendent confirms there were forty-eight residency cases over a five-year period beginning in 2005. Of the forty-eight cases, forty-seven were resolved without legal intervention. This begs the question of why Kelley and her father were singled out, investigated, charged and sentenced by the courts.

As to the forty-seven cases, why were formal charges not brought against those families? Kelley removed her daughters from the school district, so why did the school district pursue legal action? Was it merely a matter of illegal enrollment or was it more about repayment of tuition? If funds are a driving factor, which they generally tend to be for public schools, why expend additional funds on a costly legal pursuit?

Ohio offers a range of school choice options, as reported by The Thomas B. Fordham Institute. Some of these options offered include intra and inter district open enrollment transfers, IF the school districts allow transfers. There are vouchers and charter schools, IF the family and children qualify. Parents do have education choices for their children, IF they are aware of these choices. Yet, far too many parents are not equipped to make informed decisions. They have limited knowledge and don't know how or where to find information. The likelihood of the public school system working with and helping parents find the best education environment for their child, in all probability, is extremely low.

So why didn't Kelley ask for a district transfer? Knowing what I know, my response is she wasn't aware of the option. Public schools do not provide information detrimental to their existence. Alternative education programs are not well advertised and parents automatically assume the locally assigned public school is where their child must be educated.

During my term as an elected public school board member, I was constantly amazed at how situations were handled. Some are handled in a professional and reasonable manner. Yet, my experience reveals more often than not situations are handled with a *hammer* rather than common sense and logic.

Typically, the rigid bureaucratic system does not function well regarding individual situations. Bureaucracies seek to retain power and control and typically function based on a group mindset. Conversely, this case is an example where one of the forty-eight cases was singled out and dealt with individually. And the rational for this deviation was what?

No public school district in any state wants tax dollars going to any school other than the district schools. The system will use every tool in their toolbox to retain tax dollars strictly within their control. I don't blame the system for wanting to retain tax dollars for the benefit of their constituents, but who is benefiting? I would argue it's not the student, which is where the focus should be.

Recommendations:

The first recommendation is to have states' Department of Education websites clearly point to the school choice options the legislature has passed and enacted. This would make it easier for parents and families to assess the various potential opportunities offered regarding education options.

In addition to state websites clearly reflecting available education options, each school district should be required to follow suite. A template could be developed by the state to provide a minimum set of criteria. I've looked at many school district websites in several states and some are well organized and provide useful information. However, there are far too many that are woefully inadequate. They are not informative, do not provide current information, are not easy to navigate and represent a poor image. Also, embedding links is a great way to direct individuals to information.

Regarding this case, schools should develop a process for checking applications and data provided. For cases that do slip through the cracks, as inevitably there will be some, it is best to communicate as soon as possible. This communication should not begin as adversarial, but should inform the parent of the discrepancy and propose the solution. The solution should include the process to be followed for remedying the situation.

Most important is to develop reasonable processes and be consistent with applying them. Too often one school will follow a process while another school in the same district will ignore a process. This is when districts find themselves receiving negative pushback from parents and the public. The appearance of bias and favoritism is the message this sends.

Lastly, my advice to parents is to take control of your situation and ensure your child is afforded a quality education. We all want our child to graduate, have useful skill sets and become productive citizens. But we must remember: *tax dollars belong to the taxpayer, not the system.* It is up to *we the people* to ensure accountability and responsibility within the system.

Concluding Notes:

The 1851 Constitution of Ohio with Amendments addresses education in *Article VI, Sections 1-6.* Stemming from the constitution is the Ohio Code where education can be found in Title (33) XXXIII, Chapters 3301-3385.

The Ohio Department of Education (DOE) identifies under *Topics: Ohio's Education Options* the range of education environments offered throughout the state. These include variations for public school, private school, homeschool, scholarships and more. This is where information regarding the Ohio EdChoice Scholarship program can be found. Because Ohio offers a variety of options, it is critical for parents to understand the education environment their child is immersed in and whether another program might be a better fit.

The non-profit organization, *School Choice Ohio*, focuses on helping families find the right education environment for their child. They reach out to families based on identified criteria to inform them of the education options. Their website (scohio.org) states, "School Choice Ohio is committed to helping you find a learning environment that allows your child to grow and thrive."

EdChoice, formerly known as The Friedman Foundation, is a national organization that tracks and provides a range of school choice information. This is a valuable resource for parents. Their website (edchoice.org) provides an overview of the five scholarships Ohio offers. The survey data, research and articles EdChoice provides can be very helpful to families seeking options.

Valarie

Three Children – Multiple Education Environments

Why would a single mother of three, who went to school to teach, leave a safe, public school job and have all three children in different education environments? Some may say she's crazy. Some may think she is sane. However, the primary reason is this is a mother, based on her education knowledge and experience, knows she needs to do what is best for each child. Regardless of the inconveniences and sacrifices that need to be made.

Know Thy Child
My three children are a prime example of why education choice is so important. There were distinct red flags during my eldest child's early years and I could not ignore the fact that she would benefit from an alternative to public school. She thought differently, more creatively, struggled with a lot of the conformity, including teacher directed lecture things, but I continued to keep her in public school. Over time she developed more anxiety related behaviors and actions. I realized the environment was inhibiting her learning and growth as a person and this is when the choice was made to homeschool.

I have experience with homeschooling based on my younger brother being homeschooled. I was familiar with laws and processes, which allowed me to help my parents obtain the necessary resources. I was more comfortable than many parent's confronting it for the first time. It helps to have experienced people to talk to and give encouragement, because it can be daunting. Making the decision over ten years ago was not common, but now the magnitude of homeschooling has grown exponentially. The network in our rural community has increased, which provides more parents to reach out to and helps solidify the decision.

My other two children are in public school and I look at each one individually. My younger daughter thrives in public school and loves everything about structured school. She loves teacher directed instruction, workbooks, science experiments, and everything about her teachers. This environment is good for children like her. She tells me she enjoys public school, except on snow days or when she wants to sleep in.

My youngest and only boy doesn't like school. He complains about the amount of time being seated, doing seatwork, listening to direct instruction. He doesn't like it, but his struggles are different from my oldest child. My oldest child's struggles were clear and I could not continue to subject her to that experience in good faith. Personally, I would prefer to homeschool my son, but I have a co-parenting situation and don't believe his struggles are the same as my oldest child. I think he would benefit from homeschooling, but he's successful according to school assessments. He doesn't struggle emotionally or socially.

Children are different and I'm very lucky to be in the situation where I'm able to meet their individual needs and be flexible. Sometimes it's not always easy, but we do need to look at every child as an individual.

Challenges of Working and Homeschooling

For parents who work outside the home, there are challenges. I view planning as the easiest part of teaching and execution the more difficult. In Virginia, we don't have a lot of legislative restrictions and every state is different. I plan what coursework I will use for the year and it doesn't have to be minutely detailed. It's a general framework and the courses are put on the transcript, which allows us to work in a flexible way. My daughter was in the 6th grade when we began homeschooling and was able to do self-directed activities with instructional support from my parents. She had the material and didn't need a lot of intervention, unless she got stuck with something in math or science.

I have a lot of confidence from being an educator. I've seen a lot of classrooms and believe there is no single right answer, curriculum or thing that's right for everyone. When I was in school, I would get totally involved in the classes I enjoyed. I'd be very engaged in the conversation, read every passage and dive in completely. Classes I didn't particularly enjoy, I did the basic minimum. Students will load their schedule with study hall or easy classes they don't have to work very hard in, if that's what they feel they want to do.

Homeschooling eliminates the need to *fill your time* and so you focus on what actually needs to happen. My daughter is currently in the 10th grade and has tested out of high school in every academic level except math. While I still assign every subject area, the priority is math. We are able to individualize and do what she enjoys doing. For example, if she is working on digital art and wants to learn a new CAD program, that's what we do. I don't have to beg a guidance counselor to get her in that class. We simply make it happen.

Other options include community homeschool groups where parents trade off and say if you teach my child this, I'll teach your child that. I saw in a CPR and First Aid Facebook group where parents are certified trainers. Students can take a six-week class and come out with a certification, which counts as their Health and PE credit. You can really be creative with time management, the personnel used and it doesn't have to be all on yourself.

Deciding Factor

The major deciding factor revolved around educating the whole child. I didn't feel my whole child or all her needs were being met. She was getting the academic instruction, but it wasn't really challenging her. The classroom environment, her overall mental well-being, relationship with the teacher and the pressure teachers were feeling to get all students to a certain place in order to do well on a test wasn't productive. This stress was overflowing onto the students.

Fortunately or unfortunately, I've had the benefit of working in the same school where my children were students. Sometimes I would see or hear things I wished I hadn't. With my oldest, I did try to create a situation where she could stay in school and to work closely with administrators and teachers, solely because it was convenient for me. I wanted to bring my child with me and be in the same place. That's how I envisioned our lives.

As a person and teacher, I have sensitivity to the well being of a child. It's one thing for a child to do well on tests and recite certain information. However, if the whole child is not growing as a person, feeling confident, interested, loving and driving the learning, then that's not a good education for the child.

What flipped the coin for me was my child was not happy. She was not learning at a pace or in a manner I knew she could. Because I was not able to work with teachers and principals to make that happen at school, I decided to make it happen at home.

Benefit of the Decision

The benefits to my oldest child are the difference between night and day. We went six to seven years of struggling on a daily basis to get up in the morning, crying every night, teachers not being fair, the pressure and fear of doing poorly. The weekends consisted of talking about how horrible the week ahead was going to be. This was consuming our lives and though I worked hard to find a situation that would be adequate or acceptable, it wasn't happening.

When we started homeschooling, the change was immediate. The pressure was off, her ability to focus on what she loved made her happier and she developed in the areas of her strengths. When we did the first end of year assessments, she was testing out of high school level. I don't attribute this to one year of homeschooling, because it is an accumulation process. I honor the public school teachers with doing a good job academically.

In Virginia, we test or retest every year or do a portfolio. She was tested in the spring of 2017 and performed exceedingly well after four years of homeschooling. She tested out on college level for English, Science and Social Studies. Bottom line, we're just happier!

My daughter still has stress, as she struggles in Math. I encourage her to work harder or go at a faster pace, but she pulls back in some areas. That's when you employ a tutor or someone else to help teach a certain subject. You need to tap into local resources, which are abundant.

Life is easier. When we were under all the pressure and stress, especially in the middle school years and up, that was also impacting my younger children. The climate in our house is much better.

For my younger children, school is not difficult as far as academics go. My son still complains about the same stuff, but I let him know he should focus on what he is good at, be a good example, be the best citizen he can and be patient. Overall, they are doing well and in a good place right now.

Age and Gender

Though nothing is universal, I believe age and gender make a difference of how children view their education environment. Not every child is going to start school and achieve. For the most part our industrialized style of school with direct instruction and computer technology is very comfortable.

Regarding my younger daughter, she has the personality of a leader. She's quick to speak up and teachers appreciate her. She has very feminine attributes, has a reputation for being helpful, sweet and kind, which makes life great for her.

On the other hand, my son spends every moment in school thinking about being outside playing soccer, baseball, cars or swinging. That's what he's thinking about, other than going to lunch.

When we employ more developmentally appropriate practices or project based learning in the early years and children are able to explore their interests with the same standards of learning, the experience is much different for boys. Unfortunately, we are accustomed to a framework of stay seated, hands to yourself, don't talk and walk in a straight line. This is completely inappropriate in the early elementary years. I think boys suffer more with this model.

It's ironic that we require so much control in pre-school to 3rd grade. As they get older, they get more freedom to roam and talk in the hallway. Children also need that freedom when they are little, because they don't have the self-regulation skills yet. I believe it's detrimental to child development when placed into such a regimented environment at an early age.

General Challenges

My oldest child's public pre-K experience was very hands on and creative and student directed. She was successful in that environment, but I kept her home during kindergarten. I just had my second child and Virginia doesn't require enrollment for kindergarten. Family and friends thought this freakish, as no one in my circle had heard of homeschooling, except for religious purposes.

Though family and friends didn't understand this choice and were asking why she wasn't enrolled in public school, I simply stated I'm a teacher and this is what I've been doing for the past ten years. I knew I was capable of homeschooling, but I did receive a lot of push back.

The change over the next five years for my oldest child was significant. By the time she started 6th grade in public school, physical symptoms of panic attacks, anxiety, shortness of breath, sleeplessness, sick stomach, and throwing up started back immediately. It would only be a matter of time before I had to bring her out of public school permanently.

I knew of a local homeschool association, but it was hush-hush at that time. They didn't really want a lot of exposure, because I think they feared their authority would be infringed upon. However, I joined the group, assisted with test giving and other things because of my credentials. We were all supportive of each other.

The Internet eliminated many challenges. If you have a question simply log on and type in *what do I need to do to homeschool in Virginia* and information appears immediately. In 2005, it wasn't quite as accessible. Information might have been online, but it wasn't as easy to find. More parents are looking at homeschooling as an option today, due to advancements like the Internet.

I'm a very stubborn person so I view challenges differently. For example, there was some persistence from the school district to keep her in school. It's a small community with various types of relationships. Several persons called to suggest I rethink this choice. Others made offers to try to make it work, like switching classes so she's with a particular friend in study hall. In my gut I knew I was doing the right thing and at the end of the day the wellbeing of my child is number one priority. When I think what is best for my child, homeschooling was the answer. Little things came up, but nothing was insurmountable.

I've not had paperwork difficulties regarding the submission process of my intent to homeschool. Personally, I've never had additional requests for information, negative feedback on test submissions or anything like that. I'm fortunate on that front.

There are options for test submissions, which are submitted to the local authorities. It's typical to do a standardized test or portfolio assessment. I've done standardized tests for my child, but I have done portfolio assessments for students in early childhood. In all of these instances, it's been positive and no obstacles.

Parenting things such as time management, scheduling and finding your resources are more manageable now. Any parent considering homeschooling is going to have internal conversations about finances. Thoughts may include how to buy things that are needed, daycare, full-time or part-time work and who's going to help. All bases need to be covered, which makes it interesting when trying to figure it out.

Currently I'm a single mom, not working full-time out of the house and doing small contract jobs from home. As with any situation, you have to be creative in order to make things work. It can be done if you know what's best for meeting your child's needs. As with everything, homeschooling can cost a little or a lot. At the end of the day, the course work is based on a list of SOLs, which is easily accessible to everyone through Virginia Department of Education (VDOE). There's no need for expensive textbooks, curriculum or to buy various programs.

Financial Challenges

From a financial perspective, many want the Cadillac version, not the 75' El Camino. For me, I would buy a particular program and upgrade our computer. We recently took her computer to the shop, so she's been without for a couple of weeks. Many homeschool groups go on field trips that range from the local dairy to Washington, DC to New York City. The opportunities are endless and beyond your wildest imagination.

It's possible to incorporate anything you want into your homeschooling program and it can get expensive. Because of my financial situation, I focus on ensuring my child is growing through meeting her course work and minimum skills needs, which is what's necessary.

It could be scary for a person with no education background or familiarity with lesson planning. As part of several different online support groups there are differing philosophies. There's a group that does *un-school* where they don't use a specific curriculum, so every day is a new adventure. Going to the grocery store is a planned activity where they learn about adding decimals, calculating discounts and budgeting. They include life skills into specific trips and incorporate certain information based on experiences at a National Park or State Park or other activity.

There are various semantic programs like Classical Conversations, which is a very cohesive, planned out curriculum done together with a group. Some of the programs have a cost to them, but others have little to no cost. The groups I participate in are no cost and they meet regularly for social interactions, parties, play dates, science and social studies outings and things of that nature. If there were associated costs, they would be comparable to any family outing. Each group has its own personality where some have a more religious or biblical focus and others are more secular. Parents are able to pick and choose what is best for their child as well as have the opportunity to bounce ideas off of those who have gone before them. It's really not as intimidating as some people believe.

Parents new to homeschooling want to know what curriculum should be used. They believe they have to get a wide range of items to help them make sure their child gets what the parents think the child needs. It is better to limit what is obtained up front and let the child's curiosity drive the next steps. Children are going to learn much more if they're interested in it.

Personality of the parents can be a challenge. Regimented parents feel they need to meet their definition of an appropriate education versus a parent who is less regimented. At the end of the year when students complete their test or portfolio, often times they come up neck-and-neck. This is where personality may have a negative impact, because it doesn't have to be as intimidating or expensive as one thinks.

It's important for homeschoolers to be as cohesive and supportive of one another as possible. Some parents support a very strict curriculum or classroom setting and do school at home from 8:30am to 3:00pm while others are on the other end of the spectrum. It's important we don't undermine each other by saying a parent is doing it wrong, because the focus should be on the development of the child. There are many critics out there, but in the end I think homeschooling is a foundational luxury in our country, our republic, one of our liberties and we need to support each other.

Public School Environment

I intentionally left public school employment, because when I look at children I see the whole child. It's almost impossible for me to simply think about their math or language arts scores. When I was working as a reading specialist, it seemed counterintuitive to only focus on reading. Children are not reading at a particular level solely based on the literacy instruction received, because there are a number of reasons. Their home life experiences, the relationship they have with teachers, things happening on the bus. All of these aspects either add to or take away from a child's abilities and this is why we need to look at the whole child.

Like most parents, I struggle with letting go of my children to other people all day long. I assume everything is great, because I know what kind of classroom environment I provided and my expectations. It's hard for me, but at the same time I try to be supportive of teachers. I've walked in their shoes and know they juggle a lot. There's the pressure to do well on tests, but at the same time, teachers put a lot of pressure on themselves. For example, in Virginia 2nd grade and below are not required to take SOLs, but midyear tests are given to 2nd graders to see where they stand.

No Child Left Behind (NCLB) doesn't require assessments, so why wouldn't schools make Pre-K through 2nd grade as child focused, exciting, enriching and wonderful as possible. Why do we put kids in chairs at tables with worksheets? This is frustrating and I don't believe it's best for the child. However, I try to understand from the teacher's perspective the precedence of the expectations and pressures placed upon them by their principals or superintendent.

It gets easier as my middle child gets older, matures and is able to speak for herself. I continue to see challenges with teachers understanding human growth and development, which all teachers should understand before they go into the classroom. I want to let go, but I want to control things even though I know I can't, so it is a struggle. I love all my children and want them to be at home all the time. However, my middle child loves public school, which is the environment she is thriving in and so I know this is the best place for her.

Personal and Social Hurdles

As a person who is hard headed, when I decide to do something I just do it. I don't really let hurdles get in my way and there are negative consequences sometimes for having this attitude. There have been times I paid a price for being stubborn, but the primary hurdle is social.

A lot of people I've taught with over the past twenty years look at me like a unicorn, meaning they don't get me. Some ask why I'm a homeschool advocate and not a teacher advocate or they wonder why a public school teacher hates public schools. People can't really comprehend having a diverse opinion. The easiest answer for me is *freedom*. People of sound mind who want to homeschool their child should have that right. Parents have the right to choose to send their child to a private school. Parents should also have the right to use some of the investment or tax funds in the form of tax credits for their choice. If a child's experience in public school is positive and it's a great school, I'm not here to shame you or say what is right. There are great public schools with fantastic teachers and I've taught with some of them. Families and children have unique experiences and this is the most difficult hurdle for me.

My community has been teachers and when I stepped away, people seem to be unable to talk to me anymore. I'm not different, simply decided to do what's best for my child, like any parent would. Homeschool, private school, newness or change doesn't intimidate me, but it is intimidating for many. The changes I've made have proven to be the biggest hurdle or hardship from a social perspective.

One of the biggest arguments made against homeschooling is socialization. My oldest child is an introvert, so my immediate response is socialization can be both positive and negative. Our experience was negative, thus the need for change. It is a struggle to get her into situations where she is around other people, because she is shy and doesn't necessarily want to participate. However, based on her interests she sometimes will interact and this is interesting as well. I don't worry, but I do plan and execute. Based on trial and error, she has opportunity and experiences and we see how it works out.

Changes You Would Make
First, I would restrict federal influence over states' rights to manage education. We are too bogged down in regulations and mandates, the worst is assumed and people err on the side of protecting themselves. This leads to longer, additional and more ridiculous testing to protect from top down pressures. It is better to have fewer steps from child to the delivery of the material.

There are landmark court cases, which support eliminating prejudice and discrimination. It's important to ensure every child has a right to a quality education, regardless of race, ethnicity, culture or special needs. There is case law precedence, so we don't need all the other federal involvement.

At the state and local level, I would ensure teacher training for elementary school be less content focused and more human development focused. This will help teachers actually understand how a person develops from infant to young adult. Address what's happening biologically and in the brain and when children are ready to learn certain things. Help teachers understand when they are ready for certain types of activities and experiences. Too many people don't see the harm with doing certain things too early or not allowing for certain experiences.

The National Association for the Education of Young Children coined the term Developmentally Appropriate Practice (DAP). People who work in early childhood and elementary environments, as well as parents, need to understand DAP, as I believe much greater outcomes would be realized. The education system mindset is way off track with the test, test, test mentality and value is inherent in scores versus value to society. Parent's mindsets have moved in that direction, because we see parents worried about their two and three year olds and whether they know letters, numbers or can recite all the Presidents. This is not what two, three and four year olds need to be focused on. They should be working on self-regulation, motor skills, language skills and basic social and emotional development, so when they are ready to learn other things, the brain and body is ready.

Lastly, freedom for parents to be parents so they are able to make the best choices for their child. There are safety nets for dealing with child abuse and other departments to handle various types of issues. The role of the Department of Education is to educate and the system needs to minimize their control.

The *Real School* Stigma

Some say homeschooling isn't real school, but I would like to know what real school is. I began my career with complete freedom. I was a twenty-two year-old college graduate who walked into a classroom where there were plenty of materials and curriculum. I had a fulltime teacher's aide, twenty-five children and was told this was my room. The principal closed the door and completely trusted me. To be honest, I thought they were crazy. It was overwhelming as I had no idea what to do, but I talked to other teachers who were supportive.

My first teaching experience at Ford Elementary School in Cobb County, Georgia was stellar. I had a wonderful teaching assistant, a great principal and teachers who helped when I needed them. I created a teaching system where students worked in centers and groups. There were science, math and social studies centers along with a couple of different reading, language writing centers and other things throughout the day. Parents were involved and helped daily with students, which also made me accountable.

What did I know as a twenty-two year-old girl who never had her own classroom? That's why I find it meaningless when people say homeschooling is not real school. Starting out in the teaching profession requires a lot of trial and error. Parents who don't have a degree are capable of helping their child learn. One doesn't have to have degrees in physics, chemistry, biology, and western civilization to teach their child. This is unrealistic, because material is out there and no one can be an expert in everything.

Parents will also experiment and learn through trial and error. The thing about homeschooling is there aren't twenty-five children at different levels starting on day one. A parent typically starts with one child, with another one coming into the fold a couple of years later. Homeschooling is like any other process, which requires taking one-step at a time or one day at a time.

The stigma is real, to include a mindset that one child isn't as good as another because one took AP courses and dual enrollment while the other was at home. The reality is, homeschool children have access to the materials found in public school to include similar opportunities such as apprenticeships and dual-enrollment with local community colleges. Homeschoolers can finish high school with an Associate degree like a public school child.

The Homeschool Education Association of Virginia (HEAV) holds a graduation ceremony at their annual conference. Students who meet the high school requirements submit their information to HEAV and are invited to participate. Family and friends are invited and witness students walking across the stage in cap and gown. Various homeschool groups provide experiences such as prom, homecoming and dances at different times of the year. My child is an introvert and doesn't participate in many of these things, but many children do.

Back to the question of what is real school. It's a mental perception, a conjecture of what one thinks it should be. Parents need to decide if they trust themselves enough to give their child what they need or do they trust a school and teachers to provide the academic, moral, social emotional compass needed for life. I trust me and I believe most parents can trust themselves as well.

Closing Thoughts

Anybody who has even had a fleeting thought about homeschooling should look into it, because it does get easier over time. It may seem intimidating at first, but talking to others helps one realize it's not complex. One fear is parents think they may mess everything up for their child's life. A reality check is for many years public school didn't exist in America. When public school was first initiated, kindergarten was play based and children grew up to start corporations, invent things and become President of the United States. People of sound mind, who want the best for their child, really can't mess it up. People inherently want to learn, want to know more.

For example, on my child's laziest day, I'll ask what she learned and she tells me four or five different things I had no idea about. Of course, it's within her world of interest, not necessarily mine, but we're always learning, because it's who we are.

One of the most beautiful things about homeschooling is creating an environment where children don't even think of learning as work. They think of it as being, simply part of who they are. If children are in any kind of structured education, in a negative or punitive way, this causes children to hate learning very early and carry that for a long time.

During teacher training something that would come up a lot is to remember some parents will hate stepping foot in the school, because of their horrible experiences. Some parents have a wall when asked to come in for teacher conferences, banquets or PTO meetings. Why have we created a system that makes people feel this way? The desired outcome at the end of this road is active citizens, involved in community, doing civic duty, learning and contributing. SOLs aren't rocket science and if a child fails an SOL this doesn't equate to the child being a failure. There's a lot more to life!

A few remarks:
I've known this lady for many years and truly admire her gumption. As a single mother she chose to leave a secure job in the public education system and move to a neighboring county without knowing how she was going to financially support her family, yet she continues to have an optimistic outlook on life. These are BIG life changes! Most people don't consider changing jobs even when they dread going to work.

Homeschooling is reported as the fastest growing segment of education choice. Parents are realizing the broad range of support for this type of environment. The U.S. Department of Education reported in 2012 an estimated 1.8 million homeschooled students, an increase from 850,000 in 1999 when estimates were first reported. In addition, the estimated percentage of the school-age population homeschooled increased from 1.7 percent in 1999 to 3.4 percent in 2012. It is highly unlikely the reported statistics are completely accurate, because not all fifty states have reporting laws. In fact, the actual figure is thought to be much higher.

There are always pros and cons to everything in life, but flexibility and life experiences for children are desirable for many families. Many homeschool families schedule vacations during off-season months when it is less expensive to travel and intentionally interject multiple learning opportunities. Visits include national parks to learn about wildlife and habitats or spend time at the beach and learn about tides, ocean life and water sports. This flexibility allows for more affordable experiential learning opportunities.

I've been tracking the homeschooling population in my school district and the numbers continue to grow every year. Though there is a range of reasons for the increase, I conclude the two primary reasons are social issues and bullying/safety. In addition, many parents' belief systems are antithetical to what is being taught in public school, which is driving parents to seek other alternatives.

The U.S. Department of Education reports the top four reasons for selecting homeschooling include:
1. A desire to provide religious instruction;
2. A desire to provide moral instruction;

3. A concern about environment of other schools; and
4. Dissatisfaction with academic instruction at other schools.

Another factor is advances in technology, which have opened up more opportunities for parents to homeschool. The Internet allows children to research a wide range of subjects. There is a wealth of curriculum and learning tools to incorporate into and help build a schedule. Many *how to* videos can be accessed that will enhance learning. In addition, social media allows parents and children to connect with other individuals and groups to minimize the feeling of isolation and seek help.

I believe parents are the primary authority for their child and the public school system has undertaken far too much responsibility, both voluntarily and involuntarily. This has led to assumed authority when it comes to decision making in many cases. Homeschooling is a choice parents make because they do not want someone else raising their child or have unauthorized authority to lead, guide and direct decisions. It is ultimately the responsibility of the parent to ensure their child receives a quality education, regardless of what method they choose.

Like Valarie, I am an advocate for parents' choosing the education environment that best meets the needs of their child. Some parents will choose public school and that's great. Other parents will choose a private school or homeschool and that's great as well. Focus on quality education and we will cultivate a population of creative, productive and skilled citizens.

Recommendations:

My dominant thought for a recommendation is to do what is best for your child. Regardless of the comments or pressures placed upon a parent, choose the education environment that meets the needs of the child. The decision lies with the parent to ensure the expectation of a quality education is met.

Reach out to others for support so potential obstacles, real or perceived, will be minimized or eliminated. There are many individuals and groups to advise, recommend and share tools and wisdom for homeschooling. If you choose private or public school, each school will let you know what they are able to provide and support.

Consider who you surround yourself with by seeking positive, supportive individuals and groups. You will be surprised at what you learn from others and how positive attitudes can be a valuable tool to realizing success. We continually tell our children they need to be careful who they associate with because that is how others will judge or perceive them. That is good advice for all of us!

Lastly, be bold and courageous in your decision-making, because in the end you, the parent, will be sending your child into the world. You need to know what you will be sending: a child who lacks the tools and skills to succeed or an adult capable of independent thought who is skilled to think and create their own success.

Concluding Notes:

By 1993, all fifty states made homeschooling a legal option. The U.S. Department of Education provides reports regarding the number of homeschoolers in the United States. However, some states are more restrictive than others so parents need to become familiar with state data and information.

The Constitution of the Commonwealth of Virginia, last ratified in 1971, addresses education in *Article VIII, Sections 1-11.* Stemming from the constitution is the Code of Virginia where education can be found in Title 22.1, Chapters 1-25 and Title 23.1, Subtitles I-V and Chapters 1-32.

The Virginia Department of Education (VDOE) identifies the state offers public school that includes charters, district transfers and virtual education. Parents can also find information on private school and homeschool. The website http://www.doe.virginia.gov provides a locator tool to assist parents with finding a private school in the area they live.

There are various state and national organizations that provide support ranging from how to begin homeschooling to finding curriculum as well as legal support. Some of these organizations in Virginia include:

1. Homeschooling in Virginia;
2. The Organization of Virginia Homeschoolers;
3. Classical Conversations;
4. Time4Learning;
5. Home Educators Association of Virginia (HEAV);
6. Home School Legal Defense Association (HSLDA); and
7. Various parental and local groups.

Bob

A Lion for Learning

Bob is an entrepreneur and a man of few words. When you have a conversation with him, you realize he is a deep thinker and definitely a man who believes in taking action. You can guarantee the words he speaks, he will act upon. He leaves you with little doubt he has the desire and ability to get things done. His goals focus around improving upon what he believes is not working effectively or efficiently. As an entrepreneur he is not afraid to fail, because at his core he believes and understands these are learning opportunities.

As a life-long entrepreneur, he has created several businesses that provide products and services. Bob will continually assess opportunities and quickly take action when the ability to capitalize and improve presents itself. CaptiveAire Systems is only one of his business successes over the past fifty years. There have been ups and downs, but the ability to rely on his instincts and act quickly have been instrumental for the majority of his successes.

Entrepreneurship and Education

I came to realize over the years that the public school system was graduating students who were not prepared for life, let alone skills to enter the workforce. From my perspective and based on experiences as a business professional, I determined the quality of education was diminishing and had the potential to be detrimental to entrepreneurism and business.

I'm an entrepreneur in business, but also an entrepreneur in education. You see - I get it! People need to fully understand the connection between economics and education and the direct link is critical on so many levels to society.

The mindfulness of the need for *high quality, affordable* education was born in large part to business experiences. One defining point was when CaptiveAire Systems was in a growth mode. It was revealed that some employees, as well as potential employees, were not able to perform basic fundamental duties. This awareness of people entering the workforce with limited basic skills spurred action that led to obtaining a better understanding of the education system. With a sincere passion for *high quality, affordable* education and a desire to make a positive impact, it was surmised there was a need for an alternative to public education.

In usual fashion, I took action and thus began the journey into the world of K-12 education. The first venture was an unsuccessful run for the local public school board. The election loss was somewhat of a relief, yet there was a continued quest to find other alternatives.

Why Education

When asked why I ventured into education, the response should not be shocking to anyone. Observation revealed that though some children succeed in public school, many do not. For those children who don't succeed, it's going to be very difficult to achieve the American Dream; even living a normal family life may be a challenge. My heart grieves for these children and I firmly believe we can do better.

Many talk about giving everybody opportunities, but in reality, we don't. I don't like phony and had met with local school boards where some members declared they have the best school system on the planet. After listening, I politely informed them they don't have the best school system. Though public schools do some things well, they don't do all things well. This astuteness revealed, unfortunately, that a large number of students are not doing well.

A noticeable observation was how certain individual employees could not read a tape measure, which meant they could not read fractions. Initially there was denial and I didn't believe this was possible. Surely all the employees were able to read fractions, because every adult can read fractions. However, the reality is that many couldn't.

Another example is when it was revealed a particular employee struggled with simple duties. The company hired a woman to perform entry-level administration duties and we found she could not file. The initial thought was this is impossible; anybody can file. Though she was a nice person and capable of speaking the language perfectly, it was discovered she did not know the alphabet. I truly believe *this is criminal.*

These experiences and others are what led to eventually embarking on this journey of opening schools that offered *high quality, low cost* alternatives to public education. This entrepreneur knows we can do better culturally, ethically and intellectually.

The Education Journey

The journey began in 1997 when I ran for the local public school board. Though I won the first round, a run off was required because the remaining parties didn't get fifty percent and this is when I lost, in the second round. The initial thought is this is actually a great blessing, but didn't share my thoughts, as I didn't want to upset friends and associates.

The next step would be to open a charter school, which I was aware of and had studied. I had been actively engaged in helping pass the North Carolina charter school law and felt it may not be the perfect outcome, but was the best solution at the time. This led to the opening of the Franklin Academy, a public charter school. However, due to the state maximum placed on authorizing charter schools, other opportunities where sought. The overall objective was to provide a *high quality, affordable* education for the community.

There is a side note regarding the attitude of one elected school board member from Wake Forest. This particular member agreed to meet and provide input regarding the charter school application. After providing a few comments, the member wanted to explain that nobody would go to the school except a few misfits and malcontents and I had better keep that in mind. After thanking the member for stopping by, I politely stood up and ended the meeting.

Starting a Public Charter School

The first school, the Franklin Academy, has been operating for over twenty years. This venture solicited the assistance from the Advantage Group, a publicly traded company that established charter schools. They were operating a school in Rocky Mount, NC, about sixty miles east, so I made a visit and liked what they were doing. In North Carolina, a board of directors control charter schools, but another entity may run the school. The idea was for Advantage Group to run the school, so the charter was filed in October 1997 and granted in March 1998.

Early on there was some tension with Advantage because there was a $50,000 federal grant involved. Advantage basically wanted the $50,000 grant sent to them. They were persistent about mailing the check immediately and that did not feel right. The second point is Advantage said the school could not be ready to open in 1998, which is when classes were intended to begin. The earliest the school could open was 1999. Under no uncertain terms, the school would open in 1998. Advantage said it couldn't be done, so the agreement was terminated.

This brought about a new issue. Having no experience with running a school and working within a four-month window, there was no building, no teachers and no experience to open the school. Having trouble finding a building, my daughter suggested talking to a guy who was building a facility for his own rentals. We had a conversation and ended up with a building to house the charter school.

Moving along nicely, the next glitch came from the city of Wake Forest who informed me the building was in the downtown district and a school could not be located there. The result was a request for zoning change, which would come in the middle of the four months. Construction was already underway and meetings were being hosted. The first town meeting for parents had maybe about ten people in attendance, of which six of them were either friends or family.

Word spread quickly and about three weeks later, approximately one hundred or so showed up at the second meeting. Nobody in the room knew what a charter school was, so that convinced me there was a huge demand, as anticipated. Shortly after this meeting, zoning was approved and the building was finished an hour before game time. The school opened at full capacity and even exceeded capacity. There were over forty 1st grade applications, but the plan was to have one 1st grade class. Though a dilemma, this was a good dilemma.

It was decided to use the one extra room the school had rather then not open the school and turn away twenty kids. We were off to a good start. The teachers were told to act and feel as if the school had been in business for ten years, because they all had some level of experience. They adopted a robust curriculum called Direct Instruction, which is still in use today.

By the second year, the school was oversubscribed even though a new building was built next door. It got off to a roaring start. Typically, a new charter doesn't open until the next year, because the authorities want a year of planning. In all honesty, our school wouldn't have been any better off or have been as good with a year of planning. The *Bob Luddy System* was deployed and it seems to be a good method for this team.

A couple of facts to mention are the state of North Carolina capped the number of charter schools at 100 until 2010. The initial charter school law was passed in 1996, so for fourteen years there was a 100 schools cap. In 2010, the cap was removed and the state currently has approximately 175 charter schools with a continuously growing stream of new schools. It was a fight to change the law to expand the number of schools. Though it wasn't easy, there were a few good people that made the difference.

Migrating to Private Schools
In 2001, a group of parents asked me to start St. Thomas More Academy, a private Catholic high school. The academy was designed as a *boutique* classical school, initially serving a small number of students. Currently there are about 200 students with a rigorous curriculum and heavy emphasis on theology. It's not a school for everyone, but it does well in its niche market.

In 2006, the charter school cap prevented new charters, so I asked some parents to meet to talk about possibly opening a secular private school. Expecting ten or twelve parents to attend, it was a nice surprise when around thirty to thirty-five showed up. Around 8:30pm I told those who attended to go home and be with there families and we'll plan to do a follow-up meeting. This meeting resulted in Thales Academy opening the next year in the CaptiveAire corporate offices.

Four schools were incubated out of the CaptiveAire building: St. Thomas More Academy was the first, Thales Academy Wake Forest followed, Thales Academy Raleigh was third. The fourth was an independent school controlled by another group and didn't make it. They over-expanded, which caused them to phase out.

The relationship between business and academics is one where business needs academics and academics (and students) need business. When business and academics are combined there is a much better situation. Many schools struggle because they do not know how to successfully manage a school.

I clearly understand success and how to achieve it. We run my company based on high academic theories, but must be able to translate theories and make them work. This is a hard objective for the professor, so it's the job of the translator. We incorporate Ludwig von Mises, the great economic theorist. My mentor was a student and colleague of Mises, so we are close to the master.

I work very closely with Dr. Timothy Hall, Director of Operations and Academics at Thales Academy. We make a good team because Dr. Hall needs the entrepreneur and I need the theorist. The idea that business is like a little puppy dog that comes in and does little insignificant things at the school is wrong. It requires full engagement. Each side must respect the other because they both provide value. When isolated, you isolate the marketplace from a large group of talent that can make the whole process better. Part of the success of schools is the corporate team runs the finance and human resource departments, builds the buildings and lends management expertise to the school.

Everything stems from the individual and as individuals, we can make each other better. Someone may be able to make my ideas better, but our separate ideas build on themselves. That's why we'll never have successful public schools, because the crowd runs them. Business experiences this all the time. When a decision needs to be made and eight people are asked for input, it takes far longer and becomes much more complex than it would if one or two people had solved the problem on their own.

Dr. Hall brings his skills in academics and philosophy; education is his expertise. Kierkegaard is his area of interest and he's written several articles on the subject. On the flip side, I've taught him to look at education as a business.

Dr. Hall believes very strongly in classical education and in what Thales is providing. He tells the entire faculty he's willing to do what it takes: HR, budgeting, all the pieces of the puzzle to make Thales successful.

The team is dedicated to providing the most high quality education at the lowest possible cost. This is a perfect relationship and is perfectly ordered.

Benefits to Others

One of the prime purposes of Thales was to set an example or a model. Dr. Hall could be running a perfect school and people would say it's just a one-off school. However, if Dr. Hall were running fifty schools with diversity in every aspect one can think of, it's hard to deny the model is successful.

Every charter school and Christian school in northern Wake County has a waiting list. Our schools have been operating for twenty years, when very few people even talked about school choice and didn't know what charters were, but many know today. Even if a charter were on the margin or marginal, many parents would choose the charter because it's their choice. They've done an evaluation and whether it's right or wrong, they're making the choice, which has an impact on the community.

Look back a few years when there were about ten percent of students in Wake County (around seven to eight percent in the state) not attending public school. The 2016 data shows Wake County has over twenty percent of its students not attending public school. This equates to one out of five throughout the state is no longer in the local county's school system and one out of four in Wake County is no longer in the public school system. This is a powerful data point.

If the number of seats were doubled in alternative schools in northern Wake County, in all probability they would fill up overnight. As any astute businessman knows, people vote with their feet. The data supports the market making a very clear signal saying: we don't want your school.

A mother at Franklin Academy said she quit her job in Granville County and took a job in Wake County in order to bring her daughter to Franklin Academy every day. The impact on the community can be enormous. Schools have had more of an impact on individual stories than people realize. There are so many stories out there and they are life changing for many of the students. Franklin Academy has had graduates for many years and running into graduates is not unusual. They tell me the year they graduated and thank me for providing the opportunity.

Another example is a guy who works at CaptiveAire, but left Franklin Academy his senior year. The young man shared it was just a bad decision and had not done well in college. After floundering for a number of years, he shows up and asks for a chance. Given his track record, I wasn't sure, but ended up giving him a chance. The young man finished high school, is attending college and is at work every morning around 6:30am. The young man learned the right way at Franklin Academy, went astray, but is back on track and doing *absolutely terrific*!

Parental Interest in Alternative Education
Consider what some parents believe today. Looking back thirty years people might say kids didn't learn a lot, but at least schools were safe. However, schools are not safe anymore. The culture is horrific and some of the things

happening to students are just unreal and should be unacceptable.

A woman recently told me that when she was younger, she had a stuttering problem. While attending public school, a group of guys tackled her and told her to talk to them normal or they were going to burn her arm. They took a cigarette and burned a hole in her arm. She showed me the scar left by this incident. No parent expects to send their child into a school where this kind of cruelty goes on. It's unthinkable! Far too many parents know their child is not safe.

Based on my opinions and beliefs, I'll tell you public school teachers have a union mentality. Teachers tend to get worse over time, with some exceptions. A percentage of public school teachers get better over time, but large majorities get worse. Students are not getting the education instruction needed for future employment and life.

The culture is bad and education is not as good as it should be. There are exceptions in that usually twenty percent of kids do pretty well, yet culturally students don't do as well. A recent presentation pointed to a fact that most people are going to fail on ethics alone. Recently, Steve Wynn said people are not going to fail on competence; they're going to fail on ethics. This is being breed into people. Why are so many men sexual predators? Simple, because this is what they have always done, they've always gotten away with it and it's been fine. It was almost affirmed by society, but now it's not affirmed anymore. A new ballgame has been created!

Truth is many terrific, highly talented people fail. Society is being introduced to a lot of bad stuff, like all the sexual preference options. This is destroying kids out of the gate at the young age of six and seven years old. What the heck do seven years old know about anything? They are kids!

This is the last straw and people are telling themselves they have to get their child out of the public school system. Parents may not care if their child learns anything, but if their child is safe and not being taught evil things, that's enough right there. Parents can do as much comparative data as they want and it doesn't matter. The mom is going to decide the best for her child based on what she can afford to do.

There is this belief that if society thinks parents' love and care about children, society must invest a lot of money in public schools. Actually, this is nauseating. Public schools continue to cry for more money, but it doesn't matter how much money they are given, because it always comes back to a need for more money.

Look at our local public school system, which supposedly takes in 3,000 to 5,000 students per year. However, in the current year the schools took in 880. The point is the schools are actually saying they need more money because other institutions are taking students away and the money needs to be replaced. This is part of the insanity.

Instead of a billion dollars, which is always asked for on the bond issue, the schools need even more money for fewer students. In Wake County, 880 students is maybe one school. The question is why does one school for five years need a billion dollars? So much money is put into these schools, but the focus is mainly on entertainment centers.

Academics should be the priority, yet a nearby school looks more like a sports complex because the school is in the very back. There's a perception that student's hang at school for part of the day with the rest of the time focusing on sports. This is insane, crazy!

A recent focus group found that one data point identified parents do not care about sports, because the reality is the vast majority of students are not going to be engaged in sports. This clearly points to the fact that the average parents main concern is not sports. Parents may go to games and show school spirit, but overall the data shows parents are more interested in their child learning useful knowledge and skills.

Dr. Hall shares parents are becoming savvier as we progress into the 21st century. They are realizing not only is their child competing with those in the local area and region, they are also competing with students in India and China.

Parents are pretty savvy and by giving parents choices, they will make the best choice. If they make the wrong choice, they have the ability and power to make a change. Parents understand their child can attend three different schools. If a parent has three children and has valid reasons, they can be confident they are making the best choice for each child.

Benefits Received

Probably the greatest benefit is through being engaged with students and families. The opportunity to see teachers use their talents and know we helped somebody is ultimately what we all want out of life. The greatest reward is helping others succeed.

I now view philanthropy as an undesirable word. Many organizations spring up and seek out people who have money. These organizations don't necessarily want to be accountable for what they do with the donations they receive.

My son brought this up one day. He questioned giving money to people you don't know what the outcome will be, so why give them money? Seems like a good point to make.

Charles Koch mentions organizations may even be doing harm. The opportunity to actually be engaged with the school and to get the best outcome with the talents provided is the greatest thing that can happen in a lifetime. Nothing can be better!

When at public gatherings, people will share they don't have a child at Thales, but a friend does and have heard so many good things about it. Though many are strangers and will likely not cross paths again, they share what they know or have heard. What our team has accomplished has reached deep into society to establish choice, even though it took a period of time.

Creating this school model was important because it can be replicated, which will allow others to continue to replicate it. The model is not proprietary and everything the team has done is pretty much an open book. A primary focus is to share the model so it can go out into the world for people to do what they can do.

There are Always Challenges

We all look through our own lens and what I see is a public school mentality, which is the union mentality. This mentality has over taken Catholic schools and most of the private schools, including Common Core, licensing, accreditation, small class size and a laundry list of things that are not necessarily correct. Thales paved a path, which doesn't include accreditation nor require licensing. Class size is a complete joke, in most cases. Thales uses ability grouping, which is more important than class size.

Having attended a Catholic high school where there was an average of fifty-plus students in each classroom, I have no recollection of anyone saying there were too many students in the classroom. This was never brought up in the 60s. It is a union driven concept that says the smaller the class size, the more teachers and the bigger the union.

Any parent with a child in college knows there are some classes with 300 students. The whole public school mentality exists because of propaganda. You tell the parents you have to have small class size, be licensed, be accredited, and use Common Core; now the parents are saying really? Thales won the battle on licensing, accreditation, and Common Core with parents. This means they have to rationalize and convince parents who've been propagandized their entire life by this monster what is really necessary for learning.

According to Dr. Hall, Thales has a program underway to develop their own teachers. High quality education at an affordable cost leads to creating class sizes that are larger than what parents are used to even though they will come back to let you know they want twenty students or so.

One thing Thales has done to manage quality is implement a strong observation electronic system called TalentEd. The system allows Dr. Hall to track administrator's observations of teachers in order to monitor quality provided in every classroom. As of the day of the interview seventy-six percent of third round observations had been completed, which provided a granular level, as well as school level view.

Thales developed a leadership institute component to the model. Teachers are brought in through this institute and provided online training, which is necessary to fully understand the culture of the school and classical education. Teachers learn what classical education means at Thales and why it's important. Catholic classical education is very different from what Thales is doing and we can't make them alike.

The Thales leadership program also provides current teachers the opportunity to go through the process of understanding educational entrepreneurship and what high quality, affordable cost means at a higher level. The expectation is these teachers will potentially become the leaders for future expansions once they complete the program.

Regarding large class sizes, Thales is implementing a program called LiveSchool. The program allows teachers and administrators to monitor the behavior of all students through a point system from a control panel setting. Dr. Hall and the administrators are able to watch each of the campuses and understand where the behavioral issues are concentrated.

Thales is all about high quality, affordable cost. In order to maintain low tuition at high quality, Thales focuses on utilizing a variety of available tools and platforms. Though public school can do this as well, they're not forced to do so. The mission is important and we will do what's necessary to keep the highest quality education at the most affordable cost. Thales will look at every possible way to make that outcome happen.

Thales began using the state salary schedule, but has since eliminated that schedule and moved to a performance-based review system. This utilizes data housed in the teacher evaluation software, TalentEd where teacher performance is scored using a rubric. Salary increases are partially based on the rubric, which keeps the focus on accountability.

The public school tenure compensation system is grossly unfair. There are cases where low performing twenty-year teachers make large salaries and great teachers with limited teaching experience make far less money. It's insane; it's nuts! Thales is getting away from that.

Occasionally Dr. Hall will joke about the need to deprogram. Some teachers come into Thales and we need to *deprogram* them so they understand our model and what we're doing. Not all, but some and its a process.

Another initiative is the new teacher orientation, which is online. Once a teacher is given a contract, they are immediately sent through the campus course. They are made aware of the school culture and by the time they walk in for teacher workdays, they already know what Thales is about.

A model of high quality, affordable cost is not used within the public school system. The saying "you get what you pay for" is true for any system, even the education system.

Any Changes

I would get rid of education run by the government. It would not exist! There would be public education in the sense that there would be an opportunity for everybody to get an education, but the government would have nothing to do with it because it's the mob. There's not going to be any truth in the mob and it doesn't matter which mob it is.

The Future for Thales Academy

Yes, there is a future for the academy. The first Thales expansion outside of Wake County is in the Charlotte, NC area. Along the way, the discussion of having a cluster of schools in Wake County has led to having a higher impact. The model for the future is clustering schools within a particular area. A large number of people know about us and we have received national attention. Thales doesn't do anything in particular to gain national attention, but we receive many calls and inquiries. There are several articles written about Thales Academy based on us speaking at various education events.

One article mentioned expansion into Georgia, Tennessee and Florida and these might be emerging markets for Thales. Some reasons to consider expansion in these states is due to poor schools and a demand for better schools. Location is a factor, so logistically it will be easier to manage. The ability to maintain quality from a distance is critical.

As a panel guest in Florida with Jeb Bush, this was a chance to talk about what level of private schools or independent schools would it take to influence the public schools. I surmised it would take more than a third while Jeb stated it would have to be at least half. I believe the actual answer is they'll never influence the public schools, because for as long as public schools are able, they will continue to operate in like manner. Public schools will maintain their position that they were stuck with all the bad students and weren't given enough money. I'm confident they will stay with that dance as long as they can, which may be forever.

In Conclusion

Two points: education stems from the individual and they have taken an aggressive approach. As an entrepreneur I'm astutely aware that no matter how good the enterprise or institute is, they have to get better. At CaptiveAire and now the Luddy Schools, continuous improvement is what the team does. Every once in a great while there is some legitimate innovation, but innovation doesn't come along very well. It is a dynamic process, not a static process. When one looks at the history of education, the traditional observation is that it's been a static process.

I spent four years going to college. When I look back, I believe I could have done it in two years and gained the same amount of value. I believe I lost two years for nothing or at least that's the way I look at it. Not that my alma mater would be pleased to hear this, but I've talked to any number of people who agree with this assessment. Of course, I acknowledge it may not be true if one were taking hard math and science. The whole college thing is an absurdity, just as K-12 is an absurdity. Education should be a path of personal development and it's become nothing more than a process. Everything is just process and if it didn't work for you, that's your problem.

In light of the college perspective, a Thales College is in the works. Stay tuned!

A Few Thoughts:

Interviewing Bob Luddy was a great honor. I believe he truly is a *Lion for Learning*. The enthusiasm and passion he displays to help others with the blessings he believes he has received clearly shine through.

I am always enamored with the stories of successful people. Though each success story has similar characteristics, each path is unique. One thing they definitely let you know is it took time and there were many experiences that involved failure and setbacks, which became learning opportunities. Bob is no different. Yet, his tenacity married with his ability to think deeply, act swiftly and do what is right has allowed him to achieve more than he ever expected.

Like Bob, I became involved in education later in life. We all have those *light bulb* moments. The first one for me was when I was teaching at the college level and the second one was when I served on a public school board. Unlike Bob, I was elected and served one term (four years). I came to similar conclusions in that we are doing an injustice to many children in our nation. From the lack of accountability, at all levels, to the lack of consequences for poor performance, to the bureaucratic behemoth that encumbers and bogs down the system, it is criminal.

In addition, I believe there is a direct connection between business and education, yet many education professionals will argue that point. I began my career in business, so I see how the dots are connected. I am a firm believer in processes when they help, not hinder, the outcome. I truly believe project management is a critical element in education from the perspective that it's a process to help students learn how to get from A to Z, hone planning and critical thinking skills and allow individuals to experience failure and success. It is also a practical, hands-on way to learn, as I believe the majority of people learn by doing.

Many parents and people believe private school is only for *rich kids*, which is a misconception permeated throughout our society for decades. The concept behind the Thales Academy model is to provide that *high quality, affordable* education to ALL who seek an alternative education environment, which is exactly what Thales Academy offers.

The student population since 2007 has grown from thirty to over 3000 and is still growing. Thales grew from a classroom in CaptiveAire's corporate headquarters to eight locations in the Raleigh and Charlotte areas with many more locations in development. Enrollment grows by the hundreds with each passing year.

During my time serving on the public school board, I learned that performance is not a topic taken seriously. A discussion on salary schedules led me to his conclusion. The mere mention of performance-based pay brought a reaction similar to telling every person in the room they were going to be fired immediately. This is one reason why I am a firm believer in parents choosing the education environment they want for their child. When an organization isn't even willing to listen, consider or discuss alternatives to the status quo, it is not a good sign or benefit to anyone.

One claim I want to emphasize is public education is drowning in regulation, mandates and incompetence. Just pick up a paper or go online and you will more than likely read about a teacher who was caught doing something inappropriate. Administrators that took liberties in their decision-making that ended up having a negative impact on at least part of the student population. Funding abuses abound and it is true, the more the system is given, the more they want.

The misuse of taxpayer dollars can be found in every state and in many school districts. One doesn't have to look too hard to read about the misappropriation of funds or the waste of funds on a useless or overpriced product or service. Regardless of who is driving the ship, there are many dangers to watch out for and the bureaucracy doesn't help.

I agree that limited government is better for education. The public school system is expected to educate children, but they are also expected to practice medicine, feed and clothe children, provide transportation, act as police and much more. In my opinion, this is way beyond the expectation of providing a *quality education*. In addition, many school districts expect to be funded for everything they do, regardless of whether they should or shouldn't be the responsible party. My belief is there should be more collaborative efforts, whether collaboration is with other public or private entities. Also, regional programs for less populated areas would help where it is not feasible to provide specific or costly programs and opportunities.

My final thought focuses on the social reality found in public schools. There is a knee-jerk reaction to accommodate every social issue. I personally don't believe education should try to accommodate for every individual, for every situation. This is unrealistic and unmanageable, let alone trying to apply realistic costs to such actions. Education is meant to impart knowledge, allow for debate, thinking and prepare children for adulthood. It should not be a place where teachers and administrators intentionally coral, coerce and imbed personal beliefs and their ideas of social norms.

Parents are and should be the authority when it comes to personal behavior and the belief system they want for their child.

Recommendations:
I am a firm believer in collaboration. Yes, it is difficult. Yes, it doesn't always work. However, if we don't use our resources wisely, then we will inevitably waste time and money only to realize failures. The public education system should consider partnering with the local health department to provide support for the medical needs of the students. They should collaborate with local businesses through apprenticeships and internships to grow needed skill sets. School districts should work with neighboring school districts and develop more regional programs to benefit students and society. These efforts are but a few that could help pool resources, cut costs and provide for specific needs of students.

Every school district I am aware of continually cries they need more money. In some cases, I may agree, but in most cases, I disagree. The system needs to learn ways to do better by being more efficient and effective. By consolidating resources and holding employees accountable for the tax dollars they do receive, this will predictably result in improvements. This is proven time and time again in the world of business.

My last and probably most controversial recommendation is to allow the tax dollars to follow the child. Every state does have school choice, some more than others. However, each state decides where the tax dollar can be spent. For example in Virginia, the state constitution specifically says tax dollars may ONLY be used for public education. If a parent wants to homeschool or send their child to a private school, any associated costs are to be borne by the parent. Parents pay taxes to support education, but they do not reap any benefit unless they send their child to public school. Our legislators, at all levels, seem to forget that tax dollars belong to the people, not to them and special interest groups.

Concluding Notes:

The Constitution of North Carolina addresses education in Article IX, Sections 1-10. Stemming from the constitution is the General Statutes where education can be found in Chapter 115 – Elementary and Secondary Education and Chapter 116 – Higher Education.

Like most states, North Carolina uses what is referred to as Blaine Amendment language that only allows public funds to be used for public education. This is in accordance with the state constitution under Article IX – Education, Sections 6 & 7.

The North Carolina Department of Public Instruction website https://bit.ly/2zeu2LH identifies options that include

Charter Schools, Home-Schooling, Private Schools, Laboratory Schools, Innovative School District and Virtual Public School.

The following is a list of legislated programs North Carolina provides in an attempt to offer alternative solutions for parents and their children. Because state websites can be difficult to maneuver or find relevant information, the following was identified in EdChoice's "The ABC's of School Choice" 2018 edition:

1. Special Education Scholarship Grants for Children with Disabilities: Voucher program; enacted in 2013; launched in 2014.

2. Opportunity Scholarships: Voucher program; enacted in 2013; launched in 2014; and

3. Personal Education Savings Account: savings account; enacted in 2017; launching in 2018.

Michelle

Tax Credit Scholarship Program

Michelle is a stay at home mother of four, a devoted wife and the family falls within the category of blue-collar, working class. They are not part of the five percent or even the ten percent when looking at financial status. Yet they are able to send all four of their children to a private Christian school. There are challenges, but the decision to ensure their children would attend the school of their choice stems from the years Michelle spent as a School Resource Officer (SRO) and the experiences she had while working in a public school environment.

Michelle's story is not unique based on the fact that she is a believer in Jesus Christ and wanted her children to have a Christian Worldview education. Many parents and families seek this option. However, the unique aspect stems from her perspective and experience as an SRO. The impact that experience left on her led to the decision for choosing an alternative education environment.

Learning Environments
There were two main factors for making the decision on what type of learning environment I want my children to be in and the biggest factor, in the beginning, was safety. I spent three

years as an SRO in a middle school and high school, in different parts of the county. The first assignment was in the middle school and was astounded by things I dealt with. I hadn't been out of school very long, but was shocked by how much had changed, how the environment changed. I remember wondering within the first couple of weeks how a person could learn in the environment. Children are not able to concentrate on bettering themselves and improving academically when there are so many social and safety issues. Many things influence students and pull them in multiple directions. This made for a poor learning environment at the middle school.

The middle school was an affluent school and known to have higher income levels. Then I transferred to a high school in a different part of the county where students were less affluent and poverty was across the board. Again, I was astounded at the issues I dealt with. Walking the hallways as an SRO broke my heart for some of the students, but once you met the parents, the student's actions were understandable.

Things going on in the hallways were unbelievable. How could the culture decline so rapidly? Being an SRO provides a different perspective and for safety reasons my children would not be attending public school. The other choices were to homeschool or attend a private school.

Another deciding factor was morality. Surprisingly the first issue was a bigger one in the beginning, but morality soon became equally important. Being a Christian parent gave pause as to what my children would be taught while trying to teach the rules they want to comply with, such as belief in a higher power and why we believe what we believe. Concerned my children would be immersed in an environment for six to eight hours a day that does not have the same belief system was not acceptable. An environment that basically teaches whatever makes you feel good, do it or whatever contributes to you doing what you want to do is what you should do. I knew I wanted my children to understand why we believe what we believe and to keep a love for Christ, which can be difficult in public school.

Though I attended public school and lived in a Christian family, the reality is public school skewed my view on things, such as same-sex attraction. It skewed my view on multiple cultural issues and looking back, I see things more clearly. No matter how strong parents are biblically and what structure is at home, outside influences can be very strong. When children are thrown into an environment adults can't even handle, how is a child supposed to navigate and sort through issues. It's impossible!

Experiences as an SRO

Differences in environments are recognized immediately, based on my experiences. For example, school buses in public school are an opportunity for poor behavior where drugs are constantly passed back and forth. Sexual assaults occur frequently because there are many children and only one person driving the bus. The driver can't supervise what two high school boys are doing in the back of the bus while trying to be safe on the road. Yes, there are cameras and most would be shocked at what is taped and not seen the majority of the time, unless an issue arises. Looking at one issue can lead to finding twenty other things that happened on the bus.

One incident involved a student attacking a teacher at the high school before school began, with many adults present. Students would frequently gather in the center of the school, a big open area, hang out before school and do whatever came to mind. While sitting in my office doing paperwork, across the radio teachers were screaming and yelling they needed school administration to come to the courtyard, which was close to my office. I ran around the building to see a boy, probably 250 pounds, attacking a teacher after attacking another student. The teacher tried to break up the student confrontation, which is when the boy went after the teacher.

School administration had not gotten there and the size of the boy intimidated the other adults. I stepped in, subdued him, took him down and arrested him. Twenty minutes later he was fine and thought it was no big deal he had attacked a teacher. A call to his mother revealed she was not concerned that her son was being taken to juvenile detention. The boy was more concerned that a girl had taken him down rather than he had attacked a teacher, a student and was looking at charges.

Another incident involved a boy pulling a knife on a girl and putting it to her throat in the hallway. Due to an altercation in shop class, they went outside and began running their mouth to one another in front of other students and adults. The boy pulls out a pocketknife, puts it up to her throat and this scared her to death. He was arrested and taken to juvenile detention.

There were frequent arrests due to students refusing to obey commands given by both school administration and myself. Some students would decide to walk out of class and roam around, because they didn't want to sit or do anything in the classroom. Students would often come to class high, but many prior SROs never pressed charges. If students were intoxicated or under the influence of something and nothing found on the student, the SRO's did nothing and sent them home. Some were referred to school administration, but criminal charges were not pursued.

Language for disorderly conduct is found in VA law, which states persons who come to school under the influence of anything, alcohol or drugs, can be charged with disorderly conduct. Students can be removed from school premises and taken to juvenile detention. Since charges were not previously filed, students thought as long as they did what they were going to do before school, they were fine. They learned if nothing can be proved, then nothing happens. The students soon learned differently and realized if they came to school under the influence, they would be charged and removed from school.

Removing knives was a daily occurrence. I accumulated quite a collection. There were times a school would call so students could be charged and times the school wanted it out of the hallway and not press charges. It's hard to operate as an SRO within a school environment where school administration is not 100% committed for making everybody safe, no matter what. At times, the required paperwork makes it harder or administration doesn't want to bring the officer in on everything. Schools knew I would bring charges, because when a student brings a weapon to school, they will be charged. There's no reason to have a weapon at school.

At the middle school, there was a young boy in the 6th grade that sexually assaulted girls routinely in the hallway. When girls would bend over to access their two-tiered locker, this young man would come from behind and put his body up against their body. He'd do anything he wanted to do at that moment. Being a 6th grader, I wanted to first talk with his parents and school administration. It was preferable to try to deter bad behavior, because at that age many students don't fully understand the ramifications of their actions.

Meetings were scheduled with the parents and a hard copy of the code section regarding sexual assault and sexual battery was provided. It was explained that at his age the ramifications aren't as clear. However, as he gets older this is what's going to happen if his behavior doesn't stop. The parents assured us the behavior would stop, but said he's just a boy being a boy. My response to the parents was, "No, this behavior is unacceptable." There were several meetings and he eventually was charged because nothing deterred his behavior.

Another incident at the middle school involved a child who was intent on advancing his criminal career. The first contact with him was when he was selling fake drugs on the school bus. He stole his grandmother's medication and told the students buying the drugs it was Xanax. These young students were taking pills and none had any idea what they were. They bought them for fifteen to twenty dollars per tablet, taking them and proceeding to class. Being an affluent school, children had access to money. This student was eventually charged.

Then he began stealing pocketbooks, phones and anything else he could get his hands on to sell. Another student reported him, which lead to threats in the hallway and Facebook messages saying he was going to kill him or do other things. Using a computer device to make threats is actually a felony and this student ended up in juvenile detention. His grandmother was raising him, had lost control and didn't care what the school did. There comes a point when behavior is so disruptive, it's not fair to anyone to allow the student to remain.

Suicide threats were common. The first week at the middle school, there was an incident where one young man had a knife in his locker and another student told us. The school administration and I searched the locker and came up with a knife, some dip and a couple of other little things. During my tenure, when weapons were found on school property, the policy stated the student is automatically suspended or expelled for a certain period of time.

We meet with the superintendent and a few other things are to be done. The policy and process was explained to this student and his grandmother. In the meeting, the student said he would just kill myself and then wouldn't have to deal with any of this or he could kill us.

When a law enforcement officer hears somebody make this type of statement, other issues come into play. He was ECO'd, which means he was taken into emergency custody. This requires an evaluation at a hospital. In addition, the grandmother completely broke down. As a mom, a woman and human being, my heart broke. Once handcuffed and the situation under control, I tried to speak to her from the perspective that this is not the end of the world. He's a child and I told her I thought she was doing her best.

These situations are heartbreaking. Sitting there, knowing there is no one good answer. The student needs to be evaluated, needs structure; a presence in his life where he understands there are perimeters to live within and what must be done.

These are a few of the heartbreaking things that had to be dealt with daily and frequently. It did get better once I developed a reputation for being kind, fair and loving, but bad behavior would not be acceptable. Eventually it got to a point where intervention grew less. If I had to be called, students understood it would escalate in some way. Either the student was going to obey or I was going to take action.

There was one young man in detention at the high school that really thought of himself as a gangster. He was big, bad and tough; didn't care about authority. He was going to do what he wanted to do. This particular incident was after he attacked a teacher and after students began to understand I was different than previous SRO's.

Administration was called after this young man had gotten up and thrown his desk while in detention. The teacher couldn't do anything with him. The assistant principal came and the student wouldn't listen to him either. I entered the room and didn't say a word to the student, administrator or teacher. I walked over to the student, leaned forward and said either you're going to get up, walk out of here and not say a word or I'll drag you out of this room. Either you're going to maintain your reputation or you're going to have a new reputation. It's your choice. The young man looked at me, didn't say a word, turned around, walked out of the room to the principal's office where he sat down, as instructed.

When children understand you say what you mean and mean what you say, lay out the perimeters to live within and respect you, they obey as long as control is maintained. The other students in the class learned something that day, as did he. The teacher was astounded and wanted to know what I said, because I didn't let anybody else hear what I told him.

It's all about relationships in a school environment. I loved being an SRO, which was probably the most rewarding law enforcement experience because of the relationships. Students did see a different perspective of law enforcement. They realized law enforcement wasn't this big, mean guy that wouldn't talk to them. Many students came to my office to share what was going on in their life or what happened last night. I always told them their mom and teachers want the best for them. I'm not sure this was communicated effectively, but the end result is everyone wants the best. The challenge is learning what the best is, as it's different in different environments.

Your School Choice

Temperament factored into whether to homeschool or not. People trained in schooling or went to school for teaching seem to have a much better handle on identifying ways to help children learn. I do know my children very well, but want to be a mom. That is the role I choose to be with them.

Trying to be teacher and mom didn't seem fair, because I wasn't confident I'd be efficient and effective. Children need to be in an environment where they thrive and one that's the best for them. Christian school is the right environment for my children and they are thriving.

Making the Decision

There are limited options in Virginia regarding alternative education programs. However, the decision to send our children to a private Christian school was from the beginning. One or two children are manageable, but three and four require a bit more financial outlay. Also, our decision was made prior to the Virginia Education Improvement Scholarship Tax Credit (EISTC).

Once this option became available and we were able to take advantage of the program, the EISTC allowed for less sacrifice in order to provide our children a Christian education. I've made this statement multiple times that if I had to eat peanut butter and jelly or beans every night, I would. There's no sacrifice that was too large in order to make sure my children's safety and morality were maintained. Luckily, the EISTC has allowed us to enjoy other foods, not just peanut butter and jelly or beans. It's meant our family can have reasonable choices, function normally and yet still provide other things for our children.

From a financial perspective, it has massively decreased our stress and burden. The first two years our oldest son was in school the EISTC didn't exist. We paid the amount each year, which was significant and a hardship, but it was fine. By his third year, the EISTC was available.

By the time our daughter, our second child, was old enough to start school the EISTC was in full swing. We pay as much now or a little bit more for four children as we did those first two years for the one child.

Bottom line, the financial benefit of having access to EISTC is huge. Our quality of life is better due to the ability to do things we previously couldn't afford. We have fewer sacrifices and our budget is less strained. They get a quality education and enjoy a certain quality of life.

Hurdles Encountered
The EISTC is a very easy and simple application process. There's paperwork to fill out, but nothing unusual. The school assisted with making sure everything was filled out and submitted on time. They kept us informed, as far as deadlines were concerned.

Not sure this would be a hurdle, but more of a matter of prioritizing what's important. In the beginning, Smith Mountain Lake Christian Academy (SMLCA) didn't have an athletic program. Some people feel athletics is a huge deal.

Other people, including my in-laws, said it's a disservice to put children in a school that didn't provide an athletic program. At the time, I said I would sacrifice sports for morality and academics any day, which is the end result of their education experience. Not necessarily an excellent athletic program.

While it contributes, it wasn't a contributing factor when we made the decision. I was going to send my children to the school regardless. Since then, SMLCA has built an excellent athletic program. The school understands athletics, academics and arts are important. These programs help build our children into what we want them to be, so they're all contributing factors. For me the priority is not athletics, but I certainly appreciate the school recognizing it's important for some families and contribute to a child's overall growth.

Obstacles to Overcome

I wouldn't say there were many obstacles. My family is supportive of Christian education. Other family members are not so supportive. In the beginning, some thought a new Christian school wouldn't provide the kind of academics children should get and no athletics. Our decision had to be defended periodically.

I've spoken with and recommend to many parents why Christian education. We've had nothing but an excellent, positive and great experience. If this is your belief system, are concerned about safety and morality, then this is the right choice. I defend it frequently, because if one has never been in the environment, then they don't understand the positive experience.

A Christian school is more like a family. People don't understand the parent–teacher–administration relationships, which are positive and geared towards what is best for the child. This helps children make forward progress, reach goals and keeps in mind the goals of the parents. Defending SMLCA as an excellent school with excellent leadership is easy.

Benefits of Christian Education
There are two benefits, both short-term and long-term. The short-term benefits revolve around the parent–teacher–administration relationship. As an SRO who sat in on many meetings, it seemed everyone was angry, and I mean everyone. The parent, the student, the school administration, the superintendent and my command staff, at times were angry. There are many players in the public school environment, people to appease or who are trying to figure things out. Goals may be conflicting. At SMLCA, the goal is the parent's goal, which is morality and to give the best academic experience possible.

One of my children is brilliant. He doesn't have to work as hard or come home and study, his mind is incredible. He's growing and thriving at SMLCA. I have another child who has to work harder. She's smart, but sometimes retaining information, being able to communicate and put it on paper is more challenging. She works harder to get good grades, but I also expect good grades. She understands working hard is okay in order to achieve.

Though both are thriving, they each have their own level of abilities and skills. The teachers are aware there are times they have to communicate differently with her. I believe smaller class size makes a difference. Teachers that have large class sizes are more challenged to make sure the whole class moves forward at the same time, which is difficult for some.

Small class size allows a teacher to spend that additional five or ten minutes with an individual student, when needed.

Another benefit is communication. Text messages are sent to notify me about working with my daughter at home on a certain subject, which is priceless. I would argue it's more challenging regarding communication at a big school, but I believe teachers do try their best.

There are many students with many issues. A teacher might have a student in a class who didn't eat that day, but are expected to learn mathematics. Students might have a mom and dad going through a divorce and they're trying to learn science. I'm not saying this can't happen at a Christian school, but how it's handled is different. For instance, one day one of my children forgot to take their lunch. The teacher sent a text to let me know, but said not to worry as they had a lunch at the school. Again, these instances are priceless.

The relationships can't be explained to people. It's reassuring to know my children are loved. These are the short-term benefits that are happening right here, right now. Not only are academic needs being met; other needs they may have at any given moment are taken care of.

The long-term benefit is learning apologetics. They're learning how to maintain and defend their Christian heritage and beliefs, which they absolutely will not get in public school. They are learning why we believe what we believe. I don't worry about them going to Sunday school, learning something and then go to a school that doesn't have Christian curriculum to reinforce our belief system.

In public school they learn what the world wants them to learn. That's not how we are raising our children. When they learn what we believe versus what the world teaches, they understand why we don't and the reasons. You can't get that anywhere else other than in a Christian environment.

One other reason is if my child has a biblical question and asks the teacher at any given moment, they're going to receive the same answer I would give. They're not going to give them a different response. We are all grounded in the same biblical teachings.

When I was growing up, I remember struggling with same sex attraction. I confided in one of my teachers and said I don't know what to do. My parents aren't going to like this and she said don't worry; they eventually have to accept it. She probably did the best she could at that time. She wasn't a Christian and didn't have a personal relationship with the Lord. At a Christian school, I expect the teachers to give the same answer I would give in a loving, biblical way.

Maintaining a biblical worldview is the long-term benefit. I have the belief my children will grow up to serve the Lord, regardless of what they go through. They understand the Lord is their strength and can turn to Him. They will not receive this understanding and knowledge in the hallways of the majority of public schools.

Would You Make Any Changes

I've thought about this quite a bit. Referring to the overall education system, it would be helpful if people understood the benefits of Christian education. It would help if parents were given the option and know they can afford it. Everyone I talk to who wants to send their child to a Christian school say they can't afford it. I explain they can afford it, because the EISTC has made a significant difference for many families. This program gives them choice, if they meet the criteria. The schools in this area, like SMLCA, will go above and beyond to help parents.

I'm in favor of the taxes our family pays for public school going to my children's school. The EISTC program probably wouldn't have to exist if our taxes we pay were going to the school where they are learning to be functioning, law abiding, community minded grownups. This is the whole point of any education system.

It's not all about Christian versus non-Christian. All of us want our children to grow up to be incredible human beings. I'm sure the government wants children to be incredible human beings as well, which is why we have an education system. But, when a Christian school is doing just as well or better, then I want my money to go to the school of my choice.

If money doesn't follow the child, allow tuition to be tax deductible. We do pay a portion of the tuition and expenses, because the EISTC only covers a percentage of the costs. It would help to receive a tax deduction for the portion we pay. However, we gladly pay for the choice to have our children attend a Christian school.

Stigma of Private School

By looking at our last two years tax returns, it is clear private school isn't just for the rich. In fact, qualifying for the EISTC is based on income as reported on tax returns. The program makes sure people who need financial support are the ones benefiting.

My husband and I are not rich, but we work hard, have four children and I don't work outside the home. Some families have sufficient income and can afford to send their children without the help of EISTC. I make it clear when I speak to people that Christian education or private school is not only for the wealthy. We are thankful for this program that helps us send our children to SMLCA.

People who believe only the wealthy attend private school have a lack of knowledge and experience. Spend time at SMLCA and talk to the teachers. Yes, students do wear a school uniform, but there are differences.

Final Remarks

One thing I always try to say when I talk about education is many teachers in public schools are caring and as qualified as teachers in Christian schools. I know quite a few public school teachers and they care about doing a good job, given the circumstances. However, I believe the environment in a Christian school is more productive.

Having been an SRO, I saw what went on in the hallways. I knew what was going on behind closed doors. I knew the amount of criminal charges being handled daily, not occasionally. The Christian school environment is not geared towards tolerating varying degrees of behavior or deciding what behavior is acceptable from the students, teachers or administrators. Bad behavior is not expected or tolerated. Things are done immediately to counter various negative behavior issues. I've not heard of any behavioral issues and I believe it's because parents are aware of what's going on in the school. I see and interact with teachers daily and it's an entirely different mindset.

What I Know and Believe:
I want to point out that I served as a board member for SMLCA and was Chair of the board during my last year. Also, I was acting administrator during the transition period

from an independent Christian school to a school that came under the authority of Eastlake Community Church, Moneta, VA. I agreed with this move because Christian schools should be tied to a church, just as Catholic schools fall under the authority of the Catholic Church. There are several reasons for this, but the primary reason is education needs to be a mission the church supports. The church not only needs to say education is important, but be involved and provide necessary support. In addition, the affiliation defines the doctrine for curriculum.

This story is near and dear to me because SMLCA is where one of my grandchildren began her education experience. It was the first school board I served on and was privileged to help the school become an EISTC recipient. This program has helped many students and families for several years now. But, more important the program has provided the opportunity for parents to choose the education environment they want for their child.

We all make decisions throughout our lifetime. However, our decision-making tends to change and adjust when we have children. For many, we gain a different perspective or obtain a different focus on various issues, but education becomes a primary game changer. It is the cornerstone of our society, helps shape our belief system as well as equips us for maneuvering along the highway of life.

Making the intentional decision to ensure a Christian education would be provided for Michelle's children is a sacrifice, but a blessing and not taken lightly. Many factors were considered, with the most important factor being their belief system. This is not true for all families, but it is true for this family.

The SRO experience in the public school system she shared was an eye-opener. It seems incomprehensible that children in public schools are displaying and practicing such poor and unacceptable behavior, which was more than fifteen years ago. Today, many parents continue to believe they have no choice. They send their children daily, weekly, monthly into an environment not knowing what they will be exposed to or become involved in.

I agree with Michelle from the perspective that all public schools are not bad. There are public school teachers who try to do their best, help the students they can and work within a system that continues to fight against them in many ways. Whether it's discipline issues, SOL scores, enforcing policies or simply managing a classroom, the public school system is dysfunctional. Most do not allow GOD in the classroom, hallway or others to speak openly about GOD, because it's offensive to a few. The politically correct culture frowns on discussing one's belief in Jesus Christ, wearing a Christian emblem or quoting a bible verse.

Let me stand on my soapbox for a minute. I believe one of the reasons we have seen a rise in school shootings and violence is because of our disregard for our belief system. Our Declaration of Independence speaks of "Laws of Nature and of Nature's God" and men "are endowed by their Creator with certain unalienable Rights." The 1st Amendment to the U.S. Constitution says, "Congress shall make no law respecting an establishment of religion, or prohibiting the free exercise thereof." This doesn't mean freedom *from* religion, but means freedom *of* religion.

Children are taught they can believe whatever they want, do whatever makes them feel good and say anything to anybody without consequences. These assertions do not promote understanding of right from wrong or differentiating good from bad behavior. Parents have the ultimate responsibility to draw lines, provide boundaries or simply instruct children on what is acceptable.

Getting back to private school and the Virginia EISTC program. The perception that private school is unaffordable and only for the wealthy is real to many. The news frequently spouts how unaffordable education is, primarily college, but this is true for both public and private K-12 education. Virginia, a state not known for education choice, basically affords parents public, private or homeschool. There are a handful of charter schools, which fall under the public school system. School transfers are an option, but there is no guarantee a transfer will be granted. Virginia lags far behind other states when it comes to helping parents choose the best school for their child.

The EISTC, which does not allow the use of public funds, is a program passed by the General Assembly in 2012 and enacted in 2013. The program is funded through private donations made by individuals or businesses and tuition is paid based on the generosity of these entities. Yes, donors do receive a tax credit against their taxes, however it is sixty-five, not one hundred percent, of the donated amount. Even though this is a step in the right direction, it falls short in the number of children the program helps to receive a quality education.

It takes courage to speak up about faith in God and support Christian education. I applaud Michelle and her family for taking a stand to ensure their children receives an education grounded in a manner that supports their beliefs, morals and values.

Recommendations:

Without exception, parents need to be involved in their children's school, whichever environment is chosen. Know the faculty and form healthy and positive relationships as this helps to ensure you know what is going on.

Communication is key to any relationship and situation. If parents want to know what is going on, they need to take the initiative to make inquiries. If a parent's radar goes up and is not quite sure if the information being communicated is correct, ask questions, make further inquiries. Parents must take the lead and ensure the interests and concerns for their child are being handled in a manner that is acceptable and reasonable.

All parents should know what choices are available and don't be afraid to make enquiries and ask questions. Attending private school can be more affordable than one believes. In the state of Virginia, the tax credit scholarship has helped thousands of children attend the private school of their choice.

Concluding Notes:

The Constitution of the Commonwealth of Virginia, last ratified in 1971, addresses education in *Article VIII, Sections 1-11*. Stemming from the constitution is the Code of Virginia where education can be found in Title 22.1, Chapters 1-25 and Title 23.1, Subtitles I-V and Chapters 1-32.

The Virginia Council for Private Education (VCPE) identifies accredited private schools in the state. It is not required to be an accredited school and there are private schools that do not seek accreditation. Additional information can be found at www.vcpe.org.

Education tax credit programs are not in all 50 states, but the state of Virginia did pass such a program. The Education Investment Scholarships Tax Credits (EISTC) program became effective January 1, 2013. Since that time, this program has allowed qualified children to attend a private school of their choice. This scholarship is funded through private donations with the donors receiving a 65% tax credit towards taxes due the year the donation was given. Additional information can be obtained via http://www.doe.virginia.gov/school_finance/scholarships_t ax_credits/index.shtml.

For information regarding the history, mission, faculty, curriculum and more about Smith Mountain Lake Christian Academy (SMLCA) go to www.smlca.org to see what they offer in their area.

Jeff

Renewanation: Christian Worldview Education Non-Profit

Jeff is the fourth of nine children who grew up in a Christian home. It should be no surprise he became a pastor and then founded a private Christian school in Roanoke, VA. He admits he is not an expert on education, but life gave him significant insight into the education system. He believed the Lord was leading him away from pastoring and towards a similar, yet separate path. In order to be obedient to the Lord, he knew he needed to act on the calling he received, which was to start an organization focused on teaching and training children for the Kingdom of God.

Jeff will tell you he didn't set out to create a non-profit. The majority of his life had been wrapped up in ministry, so every organization he's worked in has been a non-profit. What compelled him to create Renewanation began when he was in his first position as a pastor in a Miami–Ft. Lauderdale, FL inner-city church with one hundred and fifty children, all attending public schools. They didn't have any church background. Their parents came into the church and many were drug addicts and alcoholics, but had given their life to Christ. So they didn't even think about Christian education.

Entering Education Ministry

Our church started and managed thirty-two Christian clubs in public schools at that time. The church ran a Christian club in every middle school and senior high school in Broward County, FL. As a result of this, I began speaking in the clubs and that's when I first set foot inside these public schools. As a child, I attended public school, but it was a small elementary school.

Through this experience of physically going into these Broward County public schools, I began to realize this is not an environment conducive to disciplining these young people. The children began coming to me and sharing that pretty much everything they were being taught at church, they were taught the opposite at school. These comments were being said frequently.

The move to Virginia inspired thinking of what if I can take these children out of that setting and put them in a setting in the church. A school setting where they were taught the truth all week and didn't have all this other nonsense going on. The community in FL was very poor and this opportunity wasn't feasible at the time. The move to VA in 2000 afforded the opportunity to start Parkway Christian Academy two years later in 2002. It wasn't a goal; it honestly was seen as the best way to disciple children. That was my passion as a pastor, to shape a new generation of young men and women who would love Christ, know His word and change the world. That's been on my heart from the day God called me into ministry.

I did an evaluation as to what is the best way to raise children who will love Christ, know His word and change the world. It was a no-brainer to me from the perspective that if I have them one or two hours a week on Sunday morning and

Wednesday night, I'm not going to make much of an impact. But, if I have them thirty-five hours a week in a school setting where they can be taught Christian principles, they will be changed. This will change their thinking, their hearts and their world.

That's what really compelled me to start the academy, which grew over its first seven years to three hundred eighty eight students. I realized the impact of weekday education and from there God gave me a vision the day after Thanksgiving in 2007 to start Renewanation. I didn't have the name yet, but God revealed to me that I'd be involved in biblical worldview education. All I could think of was Christian schools, but it's evolved since then. Today the mission is to give children a biblical worldview through any and all means. Christian schools are a major part, but there are other ministries to reach public school students and other areas of education.

Through this vision, Renewanation was launched in 2008. It was a part-time organization for the first three years and in the fall of 2011 it became a full-time organization.

Naming the Non-profit

I was telling the story repeatedly to others who made inquiries about how God gave me this vision. This resulted in spending thirty to forty minutes with each person and it became exhausting. I was still pastoring and doing other things. One day, while at church, I met a young couple that owned a small media company. I asked them to shoot a video of the story so I could simply hand out the video. The lady, a new Christian, agreed to shoot the video and in the course of that she sent me an email saying she had a name for the vision: *Renewanation*.

The email came through during a staff meeting, which took my attention away from the meeting and directed my thoughts towards a response. We did an Internet search of *renewanation* to see who has used it and to our surprise, there wasn't one entry in the world. Nothing popped up. This was confirmation to us at that moment of what the name would be. It was that simple as to how we came up with the name.

Belief System Drove the Vision

Without sounding overly spiritual, I follow the leadership of the Holy Spirit. I wasn't looking for a vision, but there's no doubt I was given a vision for Renewanation. I was on vacation and my church used to say vacation time is dangerous, because this is the time Jeff gets visions from God. I believe it's just a time of relaxing, so the Lord can speak and I can hear.

What really drove the work of Renewanation is the fact that there are roughly fifty to sixty million K-12 students in America, maybe a little more than that, but somewhere in that range. Approximately ninety percent of these students attend government schools that are indoctrinating them. I say every school indoctrinates children, but the question is what doctrine are children being indoctrinated in. One day it dawned on me that government schools are not neutral. They're aggressively indoctrinating children in whatever their worldview is, which is secular humanism and has flowed into evolutionism, socialism and all kinds of other anti-biblical 'isms.

This tremendous burden came into my mind and heart where the statistics reflect the church is losing. There is a minimum of sixty to as high as eighty-five percent of children raised in the church are abandoning the Christian faith. The numbers depend on who is reporting the data and there are many factors involved, yet one factor resonated. A child spends roughly 16,000 hours in school between kindergarten and 12th grade, which is a lot of time. Putting a child into an environment for 16,000 hours where they are teaching unbiblical and anti-American curriculum, children will come out as little socialist, anti-biblical people. We are products of our environment.

I developed a burning passion to save the children of the church and recognized the importance of giving children a biblical worldview. Initially, the primary focus was directly through Christian schools. It's still an important focus, because one of the best ways to give children a biblical worldview is through school where they spend all day, 180 days a year. It's the cultural decay in our country and we need to go back and ask why our country is in decay. The conclusion is children spend more time in school than anywhere else. That's why I believe school plays a major role in what's happening within our country.

Overall Objective of Renewnation

The vision God gave me, to provide millions of children a biblical worldview, is not a three-year, five-year or ten-year vision. This is a long-term vision. Over the next thirty, forty to fifty years and beyond and we're planning for thirty to forty years. We've already reached thousands. The goal is to see 100,000 new children develop a biblical worldview by the end of 2020 and a million by the end of 2029.

Do the math! If we truly give a million new children a biblical worldview by the end of 2029, those children will influence others. Let's say they only have a major influence on ten other people in their lifetime. Simply consider the numbers, they become exponential. That's our macro view, to give a million new children a biblical worldview by 2029 and millions more after that. The result will be a transformed culture.

Example of One Student

There's a young man named T.J., who graduated from the academy after attending nine years. He wasn't a biblical worldview scholar, but he is intelligent and smart. He wasn't a child who loved school, but he truly developed a biblical worldview. After graduation, he attended a secular local community college and had an English teacher that was anti-Christianity. This was the first time in nine years he had a teacher who is anti-Christian, who stood up and said they were for abortion, etc.

The teacher would divide the class into two groups to debate various issues. Out of twenty-five students in the class, T.J. was the only student who came from a biblical worldview school. The other twenty-four graduated from public school. When asked how things were going in the class, he'd say things were going great. The debates were typically over benign subjects like what is the best restaurant in Roanoke. He shared that for some reason his teams kept winning all the debates. I believe they won the debates because T.J. was taught how to think critically, not groupthink.

One day the professor told him he should become a lawyer, because you're really good at debating. The class was going well until the day the professor stood up and said today we are going to debate abortion. The professor instructed the class that if you're for abortion go to one side, and if you're against abortion go to the other side. T.J.

watched in horror as twenty-three students went to the side for abortion. He was the only student who went to the side against abortion. The 25th student decided to go with T.J., not that he was against abortion, but because T.J. wins all the debates.

The professor told the students who are for abortion to make their case first. As they were making their case, T.J. said it sounded kind of stupid. He was expecting a strong argument that would be a challenge to him. However, it sounded stupid and didn't make much sense. The first team finished, so T.J. began with stating he didn't remember half of what he learned in his biblical worldview classes, but we discussed abortion at length and every aspect of it. He started making his case and when he finished he said if what I just said is true, then the reality is every time a child is aborted, that child is murdered. As the professor did for each debate, the students that changed their minds were allowed to switch sides. Well, twenty-three students switched to T.J.'s side, saying they had never heard any argument against abortion.

Look what this one young man accomplished. Here's the point or the macro view of what Renewanation can do. One young man with a biblical worldview can go out and impact a zillion children and a zillion people. Truth always wins the argument. That's our mission, to raise-up millions of T.J.'s to change our culture.

Foundational Benefit to Others

The greatest benefit is to the children themselves and we've influenced thousands of children already. I was invited to speak at a five thousand member Hispanic church in Orlando, FL. The senior pastor interpreted for me as I spoke.

I met him at a conference I spoke at and he asked me to speak at his church on a Sunday morning. I had never met him before, but he had an entourage of thirty people with him. I wasn't sure if he had a church of five people or five hundred people. Before I got back to Virginia, they had called. My staff filled out the required speaking engagement forms and placed them on my desk. I was asked to speak on a given date at 9:00am to one thousand people and 11:00am to four thousand people. I thought the staff got the numbers wrong, which I promptly told them I believe they put an extra zero for the attendees. I was politely told they have thousands of people. The trip was arranged and I gave the speech. I have been told that as a result of the one speech, approximately seventy children enrolled in their Christian school. That's one small example.

Last week in Minnesota a woman spoke to Dr. Josh Mulvehill, the head of our Church and Family Ministry, and said she read our magazine. She wept as she read it and then pulled her children out of public school. She had decided to enroll them in a biblical worldview school. That's one person, reading one magazine, where two or three children's lives will forever be changed. We've heard this story over and over again and continue to hear stories like this.

Basically, we are helping children get off the path of secularization and helping parents and pastors get off of dead zero. I recently went to Lawrenceburg, TN to help a new school launch. I've been scheduled to go back to speak to the whole church, a really strong church. They're starting a new school where we're helping them financially, as well as motivating people in the community. I would say within five years they'll have two to three hundred children enrolled who are currently not receiving a biblical worldview education.

We are also benefiting our country. Over the next ten to fifteen years, the cultural impact and what children will believe about issues like abortion will change. There are three graduates from the academy who are police officers in Roanoke, VA. One was with us from 1st grade to 12th grade and now serving our community in law enforcement. I don't know about you, but I want young men and women who have a biblical worldview pulling me over. The value system they learned keeps them from trumping up charges for the people they arrest and the negative behaviors they encounter. I believe they will practice justice for all races, because they weren't taught racism or everyone fits into a box. They learned we are one human race. We may have different skin color, but we all matter because God created us in His image. Many have gone into various other professions.

We've already had a significant benefit in many ways, but only eternity will reveal the ultimate impact because of one life. We could raise-up the next Billy Graham or future president of the United States who would bring morality and justice to our culture. So, on and on it goes!

Benefit of Obedience

Anytime you obey the Lord, you bring yourself in line for His blessings. As a Christian, I've learned the only way to have a peaceful, harmonious life is to do what the Lord asks. I do have stress, trials and other situations, but obeying the Lord is the only way to have true inner peace.

You see He knows my life, because we are created in His image and designed for His purpose. I listen and trust in Him enough to obey Him and it takes a lot of faith to obey the

Lord. One can be guaranteed He will lead you into places that are not pleasant, fun or exciting, but He has a purpose and plan for everything. The benefit for starting this non-profit is great, because it fills great to change people's lives.

Another benefit is it took me to a new level of faith. I wrote a book called *The Life of Radical Faith* in 2014 and in the midst of writing the book, I was in the greatest financial turmoil of my entire life. From 2011 to 2013, the foundation struggled greatly. We weren't raising funds like we should and needed to refine our vision and mission. It was the greatest professional trail of my life and I was truly humbled. I had never had anything like this happen in my ministry. For eighteen and a half consecutive years, our church had gone up in attendance and money and had not experienced a down year. Suddenly, I hit a wall. I literally thought Renewanation was going to fail. It was at a point that in the fall of 2013 I thought we were going to have to close the doors.

The Lord literally drove me to my knees. For the times I was in the office and we didn't have guests, I began a regiment of fasting and praying for lunch. The Lord told me He wanted me to get so low so I would not take the credit for what He was about to do. Through obedience, Renewanation is growing by leaps and bounds. The Lord has blessed us with some amazing partners, financially and in many other ways. All the credit goes to the Lord!

One day I asked a family for a two hundred thousand dollar gift and they gave it. When I walked into the office, the executive administrator and COO were standing there. They knew about the meeting and I gave the thumbs up sign when I walked in. The executive administrator, who is a great person, told me I was awesome. I became annoyed and said never say those words again, because I'm not awesome. I led this place to almost disaster. The Holy Spirit spoke to those people and yes, I was the instrument who shared the story, but He is the one who helped this family see the value of their giving.

The relationship I have with the Lord has grown exponentially and that's due to obedience. The Lord let me walk through a wilderness and it was about a three-year wilderness. I kept thinking about Jesus going into the wilderness and the Apostle Paul going away for three years. While in the wilderness, He told me to not give up. There was something I needed to learn and would never learn anywhere else. That was the greatest benefit of being obedient.

There are Challenges

We've talked a little about actual content of what is taught and the public school system being hijacked by the religion of secularism. It is a religion because secularism teaches children what to believe. It tells children where they came from and what happens to them when they die. That's a religion!

People talk about separation of church and state, but there is no separation because the state religion is secularism. The state is teaching secular religion to children every day as opposed to Christian religion. It's gutting America of its Christian heritage. This is the primary challenge.

I have an appreciation for general education. We need to make education available to the masses, as we don't want an illiterate society. However, the number one problem with public education is the federalization of it and what controls everything is money. Based on the mandates and with money being the controlling factor, the government says to teach this and don't teach that or we'll take the money. If it weren't for federal, state and local governments giving money, local school districts could do whatever they want to do.

I actually believe public education should be returned to absolute local control. Since it's not, and will never happen because the bureaucracy is too big, then there is the need to create alternative systems. One of the reasons I support Christian schools is they are one-hundred percent autonomous and local. This means they can be very bad, very weak or very great. The parents are in control and if a Christian school isn't doing a good job, parents withdraw their child and the school closes. This is free market and I'm a free market guy.

On the other hand, public education is an absolute monopoly with teachers unions that dominate and control. The National Education Association (NEA) is a socialist, liberal, leftist organization that has destroyed America's education system.

For spiritual reasons I want my children taught a well-rounded education. Children will not get a well-rounded education without talking about the true God of the universe and how He is intricately involved with every aspect of the world. A child graduating from a secular school does not receive a well-rounded education. I'm not saying they can't read, write and go to Harvard, but they aren't provided a full education.

The bureaucracy involved in public education is mind-boggling and has a lot of waste. The actual cost to educate a child doesn't equate to what the government system is spending. There are people who believe they are called to work in public education, they're missionaries there and God bless them. I pray for them and thank God for these adults. However, I no longer want to send children there.

Desired Change

On a practical level, get federal government out and have full local control. Not local control as we currently have in a school board where they are mandated by state and federal governments with things they don't have control over. They have limited control, but are afraid of lawsuits and other consequences.

One option is to authorize a think tank to write papers and talk about best practices seen around the country. Originally, wasn't that why the federal education department was started, to be a think tank? Now we have too much central power and control. Obviously that's on the practical side.

On the other side, I would love to see us return to teaching from a Judeo-Christian value system. In a pluralistic society, the boat has pretty much sailed in public education.

Closing Comments

Don't keep your head in the sand. Just because people went to a school, played football, were cheerleaders and have great memories, doesn't mean the school continues to do a great job. I hear these types of comments frequently where people say they came through the system thirty years ago. The school of thirty years ago was, believe it or not, more secular than most people realize, but it wasn't the school you see today.

I had one public school principal north of Detroit say that before Obama took office I would not have seen the need for Renewanation. During his presidency there were radical changes made from above. He said now he sees the need for Renewanation, because of the changes during the Obama years.

If you're a Christian and want a child to have a Christian view of life, they will not develop that in public school. Actually, they will develop the opposite. There are three keys to developing a child's worldview: the home, the church and the school. It's been proven if all three are teaching the same thing and going in the same direction, this becomes a three-stranded cord that cannot be broken. That child will have a biblical worldview.

Yes, people have free will and can choose to rebel against God and do something bad, but their mind will still have a biblical worldview. They'll still have Christian values, vote accordingly and will usually come back to the faith if they stray for a while. When a school isn't teaching the truth, the home isn't doing a good job of teaching the truth and the family isn't going to a great church, there is almost no chance of saving a child. If there are two of the three, that's about a 66 percent change of saving a child.

I would say to parents, advocates or whoever might be reading this, stop letting public education destroy the future generation and do something. Get behind school choice efforts. Through the Virginia tax credit program the foundation has raised in one year right at $1.2 million. Ninety percent of this amount has gone to pay for children to attend private Christian schools. Renewanation was able to provide 461 children with scholarships in 2018. Other organizations are providing even more, which is making an impact.

The state of Florida has a business tax credit program, where it's provided eighty thousand plus children the opportunity to attend a Christian school. Like him or not, it was Jeb Bush who got the program passed and signed into law. Advocacy and working with legislators can make a tangible and significant difference in the life of a child, today and into the future.

A Few Final Comments:

I met Jeff at a Renewanation event at the Roanoke Hotel in Roanoke, VA when I served as a private school board member in the local area. Though I was not familiar with Renewanation, I was excited about attending the event, primarily because the guest speaker was Col. Oliver North, a retired United States Marine and military advocate. My husband is a retired US Marine and I served in the US Navy, so we gravitate towards events that are pro-military and support education. Col. North gave a compelling speech, but the children's choir performing at the event stole the evening and I would say many hearts.

Over the years, I've come to know Jeff on a professional level and follow Renewanation's progress. Efforts to support private Christian schools through the Christian School Revitalization Program are growing. The support includes strategic planning, raising funds, organizing and growing student populations, which are business facets most education institutions lack from a skills perspective. In addition, seeking the Lord in their decision-making is paramount, which ensures steps taken are in alignment with His will and purpose.

The Manderley Christian Camp and Conference Center located in Pikeville, TN was added a few years ago. This center is used to host and facilitate biblical worldview training for entities involved in education such as parents, students, administrators and teachers.

Jeff mentioned the Virginia tax credit program, which is Virginia's Education Improvement Scholarships Tax Credit

(EISTC) program. As an approved scholarship foundation, this is another avenue where they are able to help many children. The program allows tax credit donations from individuals and businesses in order to provide socio-economic disadvantaged students the choice to attend a private Christian school.

Many organizations around the United States focus on supporting families seeking an education environment conducive to individual beliefs and values as well as their child's talents, learning style and a host of other factors. Though this non-profit has a focus on supporting a biblical worldview education, they partner and network with others to ensure families are informed consumers. I believe this is key when it comes to deciding and choosing the best education environment for any child.

In all states there are three types of schools: public, private and homeschool. What drives or gives legislators the flexibility to propose and pass laws affording their constituents education options are state constitutions and the majority political party.

Virginia has limitations when it comes to alternative education environments. I believe the primary reason is found in Article VIII of the constitution, which has language limiting the use of public funds (tax dollars) solely for public education or state controlled institutions.

I agree that changing our culture will require a rethinking of the type of education our children receive. A saying I heard several years ago is: *your thoughts become your words; become your actions; become your reality*. I'm not sure who said it, but it is a pretty prophetic statement. What we believe and think will ultimately become our reality. If we want positive citizens living in a productive society, then it is up to each of use to make sure we are teaching children what is good, right and just.

Recommendations:

Parents need to decide what type of child they want to send into the world. This decision will determine the education environment a parent chooses. Many must try to find a school that meets the belief system they want their child to have throughout life.

I would suggest a review and understanding of the curriculum. This will tell you the value system the school has and seeks to instill in your child. Make sure you are given the ability to review not just a book, but all the material intended to be used. There can be quite a bit of agenda driven topics in curriculum and parents need to be savvy consumers.

Parents, do your homework. It can be quite daunting, but the Internet has made it much easier. Do an Internet search for private schools in your area, if that is what you are seeking. Look on your states' Department of Education website, as the majority will provide the types of education options offered. Seek out parents, organizations and professionals that are advocates for alternatives to public education.

Lastly, reach out to Renewanation to see what their available resources are that may assist you in deciding and finding the right education environment for your child.

Concluding Notes:

The Constitution of the Commonwealth of Virginia, last ratified in 1971, addresses education in *Article VIII, Sections 1-11*. Stemming from the constitution is the Code of Virginia where education can be found in Title 22.1, Chapters 1-25 and Title 23.1, Subtitles I-V and Chapters 1-32.

Renewanation is located in Virginia, must abide by the laws of that state and can only participate in programs enacted into law. The scholarship tax credit program mentioned is a legislated program passed in 2012 with eligible donations beginning in tax year 2013. This is the only legislated tax credit program in the state that offers financial assistance for attending private school. All funding is provided via individual and business donations in exchange for tax credits on their annual tax returns. No public funds are authorized for use under this program.

For more information about Renewanation and their offerings, visit their webpage at www.renewanation.org. This organization can provide you information relevant to their mission. If they are not able to provide assistance, they will direct you to potential sources or organizations to help with your search for an alternative education environment.

For information on the tax credit scholarship program visit www.vdoe.gov. It is not evident on the homepage so the quickest way to find is to do a search using the sites search tool. However, the information can be found by clicking on "School Finance" and it is listed as one of the programs under that department.

Melissa

Triplets Are Individuals Too

Why would a parent of triplets seek an alternative education environment? One reason might be threat incidents. When older students walk past an elementary school at the end of the school day saying they're going to come back and shoot someone up and parents aren't notified, this can be cause for concern.

What would you do if a stranger came to pick up your child and the school released your child to the stranger? Would this be a cause for concern to most parents? When things like this happen, it makes parents wonder what is going on. It causes parents to question not only who is in charge, but also what safety measures are in place for the school.

Safety and Health Concerns
We have triplets, two girls and one boy, and they attend the local public elementary school. Safety is a great concern for us. Older children have made verbal threats at the school, as our children have told us. I personally sent people to pick up my children who aren't on their release form. What would you do?

One of our triplets has high anxiety and is in a classroom next to an exit door that is not locked where anyone can go in and out. Any passerby can get into the school and enter the classroom. She has anxiety on a daily basis because of this and I feel it disrupts my child's learning ability.

Our one daughter has a 504 Plan, due to health issues, and there have been many challenges with following that plan. Much of her work is done electronically through a secure system, which means she cannot work at home when she's absent. She missed thirty-one days over the past three months. Most of the time she's marked late, because I bring her in to get her assignments. I'm required to make sure she completes her work and try to keep her at or above grade level.

The bureaucracy seems to have a continual need to fill out paperwork and forms, by her doctor and me. There are probably thirty pieces of paper that identify her condition, what needs to be done and what the accommodations are. I had a meeting a month ago with eight individuals and not one person could tell me what her condition is. Yet, these individuals are making decisions on the care and education of my child. For these reasons I believe my children's best interests are not taken to heart when I send them to public school.

Between the need to continually follow-up on ensuring our daughter's 504 Plan is followed for health reasons and that our children are in a safe environment, we are discussing education options.

Triplets in the Same School
When we moved to Florida, the school put our triplets in the same pre-K classroom. Based on their assessments and

evaluations, we were told the three were at the same reading, writing and number identification level. My husband and I knew that was not true. For instance, one child wrote every letter backwards, one struggled with math and the third was above grade level. They told us all three were carbon copies of each other. This is when we knew the public school system was simply a one-size-fits-all. They aren't looking at the individual child, asking what their needs are and how to address. It was more that all three are from the same house, have the same birthday and so must be able to read.

We requested they be retested separately on three different days. I brought them in individually and the disparity of the tests was very clear. This confirmed the only way to ensure they were getting what they needed was to be in separate classrooms.

Options We Are Considering

We're looking at private religious school. We want to have alignment with what they learn at Calvary. We believe it's important to be consistent with the morals and values they learn on a daily basis with what they learn on the weekends and in our discussions at home. We don't want mixed messages. The six hours per day in public school presented challenges related to teachers, language and exposure to things that did not align with our beliefs.

We're also looking at charter schools and magnet schools offered in Brevard County, primarily based on the cost impact to our family. The change we make has to be multiplied times three.

We also have an older son I have to drive to school daily, which is twenty minutes from our house, as there's no bus service. If we move the triplets to the Calvary school, that's thirty-five minutes in the opposite direction. It would take about forty-five minutes every morning and afternoon.

Our older son is gifted, which is also a challenge. We moved from Massachusetts where there were no gifted programs. He was reading the word Alcatraz at age two and reading at a 3rd grade level when he started kindergarten. He was beyond the curriculum and we were looking at private schools when we had the triplets.

But, God had a plan. My husband ended up getting a job in Florida, which does have gifted programs. He attended Manatee, which had an exceptional program where he absolutely thrived, even though it was only one day a week. He met other students who thought and learned like him and a teacher that helped them love themselves every day. To understand just because they learn differently, are wonderful people and not be ashamed of that. They can be who they are!

The public school is great for him. He currently attends a 7th and 8th grade magnet school. We are looking at choice schools, top schools in the area for education. If he doesn't get into one, we will look at private schools for him, though it will be a different choice based on his learning style, ability and needs.

Factors for Decision-making
A primary factor for seeking an alternative education environment is our daughter's ongoing medical condition. The 504 Plan has been in place since kindergarten and is very clear what her condition is. The accommodations are based on her primary care and gastroenterologist doctors and consist of things like wiping down the cafeteria table in the section she sits. If someone was sick and sneezed on the table

or left something contagious, the table needs to be wiped down. This isn't being done.

Other accommodations require her to sanitize her hands when she returns to the classroom and clean a music instrument before handing it to her. During a 504 meeting, it was recommended my daughter wipe down the table rather than expect the school to comply. Mind you, she's in 3rd grade and they say it's her responsibility.

We can't keep her from getting sick, but there are ways to limit her exposure. Her medical condition causes the stomach to move slowly. If she gets something her body can't break down, food or a germ, it sits there. If it starts to break down, the stomach stops and causes her intestines to slow down.

The breaking point was when she came in contact with the norovirus and was hospitalized for a week. At the beginning of flu season this year, I went to the school to make sure there is a plan in place and would be followed. This flu season was more severe than in the past and I really needed to ensure her teacher understood the need for sanitizing. If someone is sick in her class, she can't sit near them. For music once a week, make sure the instrument is wiped down.

Wanting to ensure the accommodations were being met, I was informed the person I need to speak with was out; no one else could help. I asked for the health homebound form, in case she ended up in the hospital again. I wanted to be prepared for a worst-case scenario and have a plan in place. Responses included people are out, no one knew how to get the form or we don't know what you need.

Unfortunately, my daughter was hospitalized again. After three days of being hooked up to IV's and machines, I did receive the paperwork at the hospital. It took thirty days to be notified she was approved for homebound services. On top of this, I was told she wouldn't receive full services because she's above grade level.

Our child has an ongoing medical condition, is eight years old, fights every day to go to school and the administration says she can wipe down the table and be responsible for sanitizing. As she gets older, I agree she should be able to do these things. But as an eight year old, the demands of statewide testing, meeting reading goals, reading books in a system, it is too much stress given her condition. In some ways, I believe the school is setting her up to fail.

After she'd been hospitalized two years in a row, we met with school administration. The words said to my husband and I is they became complacent, which at this point I began to cry. Because she doesn't get sick daily and her symptoms are internal based on our medical management, being complacent isn't acceptable. Particularly when she has a federally governed 504 Plan in place.

That was the straw that broke our family. Our daughter didn't feel safe at school and it wasn't safe. She was released from the hospital with not one condition, but multiple other conditions. Her specific condition will not kill her, but other conditions she contracts could kill her.

The administration admitted they weren't making sure she was sanitizing nor did the teacher have the right protocols in place. Her condition peaks around flu season. The first couple of months she's not as ill, so they forget to follow the 504 Plan. We informed the administration there are other teachers with sanitizing systems in place, because our other two children tell us they wash their hands after recess and lunch in the bathroom. There are at least one or two teachers in every grade that has a system and she should be in one of those classes. Teachers know the less absences, the better the learning environment. It's not about one child that needs special accommodations; it's about doing the right thing to keep all children healthy.

It's shameful and she has three more years of elementary school. She fears the flu season because of the unpleasant experiences. The average person contracts the flu, feels bad for a day or two, takes some medicine, and it passes. Her experience is she couldn't breathe, swallow, feel anything in her stomach, rushed to the emergency room and hospitalized for several days. Her mindset has been damaged to a degree where we are trying to build happy memory responses, even though it would be fake memory when flu season starts.

Homebound and Assessed Learning Level

Homebound is when the school district provides a certified teacher to give instruction at home either intermittently, partially or full term. For us, it required medical documentation where the doctor indicates what is needed. The administration makes their decision based on the information provided and individual academics. Regardless of what is submitted, the school decides what will be provided. Since our daughter is above grade level, they only authorized what they believe will be sufficient for her grade level.

As the parent, I don't agree with their decision. The administration came up with a plan different from what her doctor says she needs. No one making the decision is a doctor nor do they understand her medical condition. When questioned, I was informed there's a shortage of teachers able to provide homebound services. They try not to allocate time to children who are above grade level. In essence, she is penalized because I work with her to keep her above grade level.

Common core standards have gotten to a grade level where I don't know how to do the math or social studies the way they are teaching. If someone asked me to calculate twelve minus seven, I would say it's five. I would not truncate, break off, do ten and a two; then multiples of five are two so this would be five and bring down the two and add five plus two equals seven. I'm not familiar with this way of teaching.

We consider ourselves a responsible family and don't abuse the system. When she feels better, regardless of the time, I take her to school so she can ask questions and catch up. I believe we're being penalized. There are people who abuse the system and I understand that. On the other hand, a homebound child with medical documentation, provided by a doctor, should not be denied services or provided less because she's above grade level.

Challenges Faced
The biggest challenge leaving the school system would be the social transition. They're in the 3rd grade and have been with the same group of children for four years. Our triplet son is a very social child and would miss recess and playing sports with his friends. The girls have each other so they can play girl things and get social input. It would be a little more challenging to make sure I'm finding programs or play groups that meet his needs.

If the children remain in public school, which we're still trying to work through, the challenge is safety. We need to ensure her health needs while at school don't become complacent. That her health is as important to them as it is to us. Parents deal with peanut allergies at schools, we communicate and it's not a problem. Some children are diabetic, need insulin and this doesn't seem to be an issue.

Our daughter has a very uncommon medical condition. Her medication is not on an approved list and we had to fight to ensure she is able to take her medication while at school. One day I was called by a nurse supervisor and told it would be removed from her person even though the doctor authorized her to self-medicate. The school didn't have a full time nurse and she wasn't able to get her medication any other way. It became a battle. I told them if they took it from her I would call law enforcement, because her medication is lifesaving. She needs it when she needs it, just like a diabetic. I'm sorry it's not on an approved list.

Another challenge is people need to educate themselves. When you're an administrator, like in any job, there will be unfamiliar situations encountered. Whether at a large pharmaceutical company or a small department store, there will be times when something you've never dealt with happens. Throwing your hands up, doing nothing, is not the solution. It's unfortunate this happens.

Obstacle to Overcome
The primary obstacle is my autoimmune condition, which is one reason I don't consider homeschool. I need to take care of myself so I can be around long-term for my children.

I don't work outside the home because of my medical condition and caring for our children. People shouldn't be required to divulge private medical information to receive lawful services or be treated fairly. My medical condition has nothing to do with my daughters 504 Plan. I do what I have to do to care for our daughter, when needed, and myself.

My husband is worried about my health and doesn't want to consider homeschool either. I'm not sure how I would manage having the children home all day, as I need my rest during the day. However, it would make grocery shopping more interesting, having three additional people with me all the time.

Benefits for My Children

One benefit is the way they look at school. I imagine it would be more positive. Every afternoon I pick them up, the first thing out of their mouth is a negative. So and so said a swear word or used language they shouldn't have or someone hit somebody. Someone said something mean to someone else about the way they look or what they were wearing. This is such a negative environment. My husband and I don't recall this behavior in 3rd grade. What we remember is going to school, having fun and playing with our friends. Yes, things did happen, but we were in middle school by then and understand more of right and wrong and how to treat others.

Good character is what we are trying to instill in our children. We want to help them develop into human beings who are good to others. It seems the six hours they spend at school, the things they encounter, are negative. Teachers resort to yelling, because of the stress. Again, this is not what they should be dealing with. School should be a fun environment that children look forward to.

We go to Calvary Chapel on Sundays. The children are in ministry for two hours and come skipping out. They want to share what they learned, tell us all about the message and what we need to do for the week. They share what they should focus on and the games they played to help make us better people. They share about the programs going on in our community that help others or support one another. They're happy. We frequently have to ask each of them to speak one at a time.

When they come home from their current school the focus is on homework, study for a test or read this book, which they don't want to read. Life is too short and before we know it they will be adults with jobs and responsibilities. Let them enjoy childhood; enjoy life. They should be with friends, building friendships and becoming good people, good adults. They are our future and I find it sad. Our children deal with negativity on TV, at school and in society. So, we're concerned with where their life path will lead them.

What Makes a Difference?

Teachers' attitudes make a difference. Parents aren't held accountable for things their children do and will say kids are kids or they are busy with work and the stresses of life. I agree there are more stresses, but I know I'm accountable. If my child goes to school and stabs someone with a pencil, I'm as accountable as my child. They should know better and I wouldn't say, "Well, he's a child."

Based on my observations, I'd say it's fifty-fifty that some teachers still try to be caring. Some teachers teach right from wrong, but children go home to parents that don't have the same definition of right and wrong, so poor behavior remains in the school. The flip side is some teachers are burnt out from battling and correcting poor behavior all day, which adds to their stress. I had a teacher tell me a student stood up in her classroom and said, "Everybody stop talking, shut the f... up" and she laughed. She did not send the child to the principal's office or call the parents. I told her this is not appropriate language for the classroom.

The teacher is not sending a message to students or parents that it's unacceptable, so the behavior continues. People must be held accountable. It's hard; no one wants to be the bad guy, but parents made the choice to have a child. We made a choice, we're a very busy family and my children will tell you we hold them accountable even though they don't always like it. I'm not always the good guy and they don't like me getting angry, but it's my job. Being a parent isn't an easy job.

I believe it's a hard place right now in public schools with so many laws changing over the years. People worry about being sued or the reputation they have in the community due to a change in the discipline policy. Standing up against someone doing something you know is wrong is difficult. However, I don't have a solution on how to fix it.

My older son is turning thirteen. The three and a half years between when he finished elementary school and the triplets starting is night and day. I think about what the next three and a half years is going to bring and I find it scary.

One example is using a swear word or bad language in the classroom. My son said that would never have happened when he was in 3rd grade. If a child did say a swear word the teacher would have the child sit in the hall or go to the principal's office. There were consequences and children knew it. It's difficult for teachers to manage multiple students with disruptive behavior versus the one off.

My older son doesn't remember all the difficult homework or stress of statewide testing. There was no statewide testing when he was in 3rd grade. The state tells us it's to improve student achievement, but I fail to understand how a 3rd grader given two days of testing for reading and two days of testing for math is better. What this does cause is anxiety.

Children are expected to do well. Portfolios are created to show poor results and there are ways to determine if there is a one-off. Why not take the test and move on, they either know it or don't. Children need to be allowed to be kids.

I grew up taking standardized tests, but it wasn't such an important factor in my education experience, like it is today. I showed up at school and told today is the test. Everyone would put their things away, get their pencil, color in the little dots and that's the last I heard of it. I don't remember asking my mother if I passed or what my grade was. Teachers didn't teach to the test. They didn't say we're going to do additional work so if you fail it, there's a net. The test was given, it didn't stress me out and I went about my day.

Three years ago my son didn't have to worry about this, thank goodness. He doesn't like them now that he's in the 7th grade and believes he would have failed in the 3rd grade.

They're forcing children to grow up and do more and more. Children are missing the simple things we all learned thirty years ago or even three years ago. We did our schoolwork, but also learned about how to be a good friend, be humble, kind and how to help someone struggling on a math test. Now if you try to help someone, you get in trouble for talking. There's a push to get through more and more. If one is struggling and another is above grade level, we can't help because we have to go, go, go.

It's important to build character. Good character will get you further in life than a ninety or one hundred on a state test. We're missing the fundamentals of human kindness. Children don't learn good character and this is why private schools, especially schools like Calvary Chapel, build these into the curriculum. Life isn't all about a math test, learning science or social studies. As children grow, seeds get planted and hopefully they grow into very kind, loving, caring adults.

Changes You Would Make
I would say the administration. What I mean is the school board and the local Brevard County administration team in central office. From my knowledge, I believe administrators are often times individuals who are removed in that they don't have children in school. For instance, a couple of people in our school system have children in college and I'm not sure they understand the challenges families face today. Some don't seem to understand what children are exposed to with apps, video games, guns and violence. People are busy and will often use electronics as babysitting tools. There's inconsistency between today's society and decision-making.

For example, my children are on the computer at school doing reading, math and taking tests. Then they do more on the computer with reading and homework. Studies show there should be screen-time limitations for their age. They are well over the amount of screen-time at school, let alone doing more at home. I believe overuse of electronics is detrimental to learning, brain development and how they function over the long-term. Again, children need to be kids. To get out and play with others helps them develop problem-solving skills and learn to work as a team.

Some of my friend's children don't do activities because of the amount of homework. They get home and do homework from 3pm to 8pm because their child might be struggling in a specific area. We seem to forget part of the growing process includes time for the brain to unwind, relax, take in some fresh air, run around and be silly.

Drive time is another thing I would change. We don't have buses or middle schools in our area, so parents are driving their children to middle schools all around the county. This puts us home around 5pm, which is dinnertime for many families. Then we're off to activities. Our family time is basically on weekends, because our older son gets home late in the day. He does his homework and by the time he's finished, his younger siblings are getting ready for bed. Family bonding and family time is so important.

Let's get back to the school board. I know we vote, but if we don't have people running for public office, there's no choice. One school board member stated in a meeting they have been fighting for a middle school since their child was in elementary and now they're in college. We've been in the area five years. I admit I was a little shocked the individual was still on the school board fighting the same battle. I'm not sure they're fighting for the needs of children today.

School board members should visit schools so they can see the challenges. Walk into the public school and see it is wide open. Walk in like a parent, look around, come through the back door and address the issues. Don't simply say they saw problems, but not address them or send out a survey. There has not been a middle school in Viera since we've lived here, yet the survey continues to ask the same question. They don't appear to be doing anything about resolving the issue. I'm not sure it's a priority, from a parent's perspective.

Regarding the survey, it's sent out electronically and I'm not sure the school board takes the results seriously. I've personally attended meetings and spoken to members about travel time to take children to school. I've shared the challenges with homework and tutoring, which is not offered at schools anymore. The stress on children and families is enormous. Children race home to get on the computer to get homework done so they can get to their activity and be a child.

I realize my perspective is unique because we do have four children. Even parents with one or two children say they can't have their child in anything. It's too much to even have a half hour of down time. For parents who work two jobs – forget it.

Final Comments

Public schools do have their negatives, but I don't discourage people from sending their children to public school. I believe it's about choices and what's right for our family may not be right for another family. We are grateful Florida has choices such as charter schools. Children can go from one public school to another, as long as there is room. As I mentioned, we moved from Massachusetts where we didn't have these choices. You went to the assigned school, take it or leave it. You can go to a private school, but this isn't really an option for many.

With our older son we have nothing negative to say about the public schools or his experiences in them. It's a good fit for him, but in wasn't in Massachusetts. So each situation and each child is different, just as each family needs are different.

Our particular situation with our triplets in public school has not been as great an experience as we had hoped. I'm not saying middle school or high school won't be different. They will be older and able to advocate and speak for themselves. If we do move them to Calvary Chapel, we've discussed going into high school. That decision will be made as we move further along the path. Every year changes: children change; family needs change; the school system changes.

My Three Cents:

Melissa, like all good parents, is engaged in the education of her children. Whether you agree with her or not from a faith perspective, all parents should be concerned and advocate for the safety and health of their children. I applaud her for voicing her concerns at the elementary school her triplets attend.

I have no experience with medical issues, certainly not with my children. Sending your child to a building five days a week that appears to have a flippant or cavalier attitude towards one of your most prized possessions is maddening. When the illness is life threatening, I'm confident in saying this has a compounding effect.

Many children in the public education system have a 504 Plan, which is governed by the Rehabilitation Act of 1973. Part of the process for developing this plan includes a medical evaluation performed by a medical professional to determine the condition. Schools are obligated to follow the evaluation recommendations. Unfortunately, I've had many parents share with me that their child's plan is not followed, which is a violation of law. The bureaucracy often quickly overwhelms parents, but they must not lose heart. They are the best advocate for their child and need to stay engaged and demand the conditions identified in the 504 Plan be met.

Melissa and her family are seeking alternative education environments for their triplets, which is what parents should do if they are not satisfied with their current situation. Fortunately, Florida has several alternatives to consider, unlike Massachusetts where they previously lived. When parents know there are alternatives, they can evaluate each one, which empowers them to make informed decisions. Not only is this good for the child, it is good for the education system.

I'm a person who believes competition is good and find competition for the education system to be of great value. Education is a business and it is BIG business. We must acknowledge that government controlled education is a monopoly. When a monopoly is confronted with competition, there is typically one of two results. The first is resistance and the second is improvement. If we truly seek improvement in the education of our children, we need to encourage and embrace competition.

It is clear to see that Melissa and her family are looking out for the best interests of their children. The older son is in a public school gifted program, which is what he needs. The triplets are not as fortunate.

Recommendations:

Parents, if you have children with a 504 Plan, you must become familiar with the Rehabilitation Act of 1973. It is a boring and daunting read, but if you are to advocate for your child, you need to know what your rights are. Otherwise, legal assistance may be necessary.

Get to know the individual or administrator within the education institution who manages the various disability programs. Work with them closely to ensure all requirements are being met. If there are discrepancies, bring them to the attention of the individual or administrator and set deadlines for remedies and solutions. Remember, you are the best advocate for your child.

Reach out to your elected representatives, both local and state. If they are not able to provide immediate recommendations, they should be able to point you to individuals, offices and organizations that will be able to help or provide assistance.

Network with other parents as there is strength in numbers. Remember you are not an island and there are other parents in your area who struggle with ensuring their child is accommodated in accordance with the law.

Concluding Notes:

The Rehabilitation Act of 1973 and Individuals with Disabilities Education Act (IDEA) is federal legislation that serves students with special needs. Though these pieces of legislation are not the same and vary in what is allowable, all public schools are required to identify, report and provide appropriate public education to eligible students with disabilities. However, some students with disabilities do not quality under this act. Parents must take an active role, familiarize yourself with the law, know your rights and advocate for your child.

The Constitution of the State of Florida was revised in 1968 and subsequently amended. Article IX – Education consists of 8 Sections, which provides the foundation. Additional policy is found under Florida statute Title XLVIII – K-20 Education Code, Chapters 1000-1013. The document is located at http://flsenate.gov/Laws/Constitution.

The Florida Department of Education (DOE) has a consumer friendly website and identifies the various programs for K-12 education under the K-12 Public Schools section. The website http://www.fldoe.org/schools/school-choice/ is one of the best and most informative when it comes to seeking information on the options the state offers for education environments. Parents will find information relating to scholarships, private schools, charters schools, virtual education and more.

The non-profit *Step Up for Students* in Florida helps parents navigate five scholarships the state offers. This organization offers assistance through identifying the best program for a child or finding other statewide and local resources based on learning needs. The website is https://www.stepupforstudents.org.

Denisha

Saved by a Scholarship

Dreams should be big, otherwise why dream! As a little girl from the south side of Jacksonville, FL, Denisha had little hope of graduating from high school like many children in a similar environment. Yet, for some reason she was singled out and literally saved by a scholarship because of the actions of a Good Samaritan. Some don't believe in fairy tales or happy endings, but she rose from her inner city life to become a guest of the President of the United States in February 2017.

A Rough Start
I will begin by saying my mother gave birth to me at the age of sixteen, a child having a child. Often she left me at different friend's houses and the mother of one friend became my godmother. At the age of three months is when I was thrust into my godmother's life. Over the years, she sought legal action to try to obtain full custody, but was unsuccessful. At the age of thirteen I told my mother I didn't want to live with her anymore and that's when I went to live with my godmother permanently.

Prior to this life change, I was not doing well in school. We lived in hotel rooms or with friends and life was not good. I attended neighborhood public schools and the constant moving had a negative impact on my academic performance. I attended five different elementary schools and they were all in low-income areas. Most of the students lived in poverty, like us, and it was difficult. Though I now know differently, teachers didn't seem to have enough energy to care. As a child, we don't realize or understand how much teachers do.

Academically I was failing as I couldn't read, do math or do a lot of subjects. I remember reading in class was very painful. I literally hated it and cried while reading. The teacher's would tell me I needed to work on reading and move on to the next student. Consequently, I failed the 3rd grade twice. The first time I failed was because Florida law states that if you don't pass the standardized test, you either attend summer school or are held back. I didn't pass the reading exam. My life situation was so bad I didn't do summer school, so I had to repeat the grade.

In 4th grade I was enrolled in the STAR program, which was for students like myself, who failed multiple times. There were students in the class who were two, three and four grades behind and I couldn't even pass the *dummies* class. It really wrecked my self-esteem, knowing I couldn't even succeed in this program.

By the time I was in the 5th grade, I had thrown up my hands and knew school was awful. I wasn't succeeding, so why should I care. I was getting into fights, going to school in my pajamas and life was not good. Though I did attend school, I missed many days. I didn't feel obligated to go to school, because my biological mother would let me miss, regardless of the excuse. As a child, I was perfectly fine with staying home.

At the age of thirteen, I was entering the 6th grade and began living with my godmother, who is a faith-believing woman and so am I. She always took me to church on Sundays when I was at her house on the weekends. By the time I began living with her full-time, the church opened a school, which she thought was perfect. I agreed because all my friends from church went to the school, but she didn't have a way to pay for private school. Fortunately, someone told her about a scholarship and that's how I started at Esprit de Corps.

The Scholarship Program
It was 2002 and in the 6th grade when I started the *Step Up for Students* scholarship program, the only program available at the time. This scholarship provides opportunity for low-income families to send their child to a private school. I believe Florida now has additional scholarship programs.

The scholarship is a tax credit program funded by private donations. Corporations and individuals can donate dollars and receive a tax credit. In addition, things like old cars can be donated and the dollar amount received goes toward the scholarship.

Dramatic Life Changes
When I began living with my godmother, my life was in shambles, both in and out of school. However, she provided me with a stable life. We had moved into a Habitat for Humanity home and realized the Police Athletic League (PAL) was behind the house, so I began to go there after school. She really thought about my future and developed a plan for what my life was going to include.

The neighborhood public school was underperforming and families were living in poverty. The move did not take me out of poverty into middle class. I went from living on the east side of Jacksonville to the north side, which wasn't much better. There wasn't a big difference from an income perspective and the schools weren't much better.

Though we struggled financially, she knew this private school was going to be our best hope. She's a social butterfly, so she told everybody about me attending the school. If she didn't get the scholarship, I'm sure she would have found an alternative source to fund my academics. This was a different mindset from my biological mother who didn't care about my academics, where my godmother from day one cared about everything.

At Esprit de Corps I felt a difference with the teachers. From day one they were at the door smiling and hugging and I thought it was weird. On the first day it can be expected, because it's a new school. Teachers on every first day are bright-eyed and bushy tailed, but I didn't think they would stay like this forever. I expected to show up, be my normal self, be disruptive and turn the teachers off, but this never happened. Every morning the teachers continued to be at the door smiling and hugging.

One thing was the same in that I was expected to read in the classroom. At my previous schools, I read and cried through sentences. Teachers would dismiss me, let somebody else read and tell me I needed to practice reading. However, at the private school I would read and cry, but the teachers would not move to the next person. They would have me continue reading while sobbing and crying, stumbling over words and they would not move on to another student. The teacher would ask who wanted to read next and students would raise their hand, but not me. Teachers would call on me even though I didn't want to read, but they would insist. I thought they were picking on me, because that's what happened in other schools. Students would snicker in the background when I would pronounce a word incorrectly. I soon realized other students were not snickering, the teachers were not snickering and no one was laughing.

As they continued to call on me, my reading improved. I wouldn't cry anymore or stumble over words. This was such a relief. After a time I noticed I wasn't being called on as much to read aloud. Though I didn't understand it at the time, in the end they were helping me improve.

During summers, students would go over to teacher's houses and they would help us with multiplication tables. We would read together or sit at the table and teach us table etiquette. These were hands-on lessons I'd never experienced with any teacher before. Public school teachers would retreat into the teacher's lounge and you would see the disgrace on their face when they came back into the classroom. At Esprit the teachers ate with us, wouldn't leave us alone and actually liked us. At first, it seemed weird and I didn't like it, but after a while, they didn't break. The teachers and students were consistently nice, kind and loving. At first, it was a real culture shock and I didn't know what was going on. I have to admit I didn't like it sometimes.

I finally realized this is good and they were not going to change. I always expected change in the other schools I went to. Initially, teachers were nice, but not for long. The teachers at Esprit didn't do that; they didn't change. They were consistent until the day I graduated.

My Godmother's Choices

My godmother is in her seventies, has four biological grown children and all had graduated by the time I began living with her. Her first child died a victim of drugs and the streets. The second child is married, a truck driver, has a family and is successful. The third and fourth are doing well. Each one is unique and very different. By the time I moved in she had years of experience and knew what was needed.

She truly is a saint! She adopted three younger children after I was in the 8th grade and was a foster parent for most of my childhood. I believe I was really important to her and she knew what I needed. Because she had already raised children, I believe it was a little easier for her to recognize the unique needs I had at the time.

Interesting, I have never looked at it from this perspective. Knowing she raised four biological children and what she learned from life experiences. How this lead to the decision to take me in and care about my education.

During my public school years if someone told me I had to make good grades, I would have asked why. When I attended the small private Christian school, they would tell me I had to make good grades. When I asked why, they told me because you have to do everything unto the Lord with excellence.

I didn't know how to spell my last name for the longest time because it's so long, so I simply wrote Denisha M. My godmother sat me down and had me write my name so many times. I wrote it sloppy and she would tell me to write it neat. I asked why and she would say you do everything with excellence as if the Lord were looking at it. She told me that all the time. I would get so upset, but it was true. My godmother and the school knew writing my name is not just for me. It's for something higher, because they believe God is looking, watching. You have to acknowledge this about many things in life such as the things we wear and how we act, because it's not all about me.

What I Overcame

As I previously identified, my biological family was high poverty and low responsibility. Most have not graduated from high school, as education is not a priority. It's never been viewed as something to help you succeed in life. The focus is always on something else, such as being a good basketball player might get you into the NBA. If you can hustle, you can make a living selling drugs. Education is not viewed as a path to becoming a doctor and earning a good living. It's a different mindset and perspective.

Once I began making good grades, I became different socially and began to share my story. This is where I really had to focus on faith building. Honestly, my godmother would say things like, "I know you love your mother, but this is your truth." I knew I loved my family, but what they were saying shouldn't matter.

For example, a stereotype of if you like books, you like to learn and so you're a nerd or trying to be white. Another example is because you want something different, you're forgetting about your people. That was difficult for me to deal with as a child. I didn't have people around me who made good grades and cared about school. People who cared about living a good life and not a life of fear every time a certain car drove down the street. This was different and a challenge for me.

To be honest, I still struggle with this today. Even now in my position, the understanding still isn't always there as to why it's so important to be a good citizen and appreciate knowledge.

Mindset Shift
Some in my family have an entitlement mentality where they tell me I'm doing well, so come and help us. They tell me that I'm a big shot and so I must give to them or do for them or whatever.

I don't think about being sucked back into my old life. To be honest, I don't think about drifting back into the old mindset, because I left it behind. I'm not sure why, but I guess avoidance is the best solution to everything. Just kidding! I know different now and am grateful for where I'm at in my life.

Greatest Obstacle to Overcome
It goes back to the emotional intelligence piece. As a child, education was never really appreciated. When I started attending the private school, I still didn't appreciate education. However, I had a wake-up call moment. My attitude in public school was really crappy and when I started attending private Christian school I didn't automatically turn into a rosebush. It took time and people were really patient with me.

I received in-school suspension (ISS) in the 6th grade, which was normal behavior for me, but not normal behavior at Esprit; the students were different. ISS is normal behavior in public school as most students who were disruptive eventually received detention and were sent to the principal's office. At Esprit this was not the norm and only about one percent of the students were disruptive.

My behavior rewarded me with ISS and the man doing ISS was a member of the church. I had this bipolar switch because at church, I was an angel and they were not familiar with the Denisha they saw at school. They wondered who this person was with such bad behavior. Anyway, the man was a deacon and a big buff guy who served in the military and was a firefighter. So this big, buff guy tells me that if I don't get my act together, I'm going to end up in jail and I just start crying. To this day, I tell him I really don't know why that hurt me so bad, but it hurt. That was my wake-up call.

That experience was the switch that made me stop and think. It was difficult, but in that moment, I realized I had to stop. I can't fault anybody, can't make excuses, it was up to me to change my behavior and that was hard. This is the point when my attitude changed, began to appreciate education and all the teachers who were trying to help me. I went on to get bachelor and master degrees. I don't think I'll do a doctorate though.

Benefits of My Decision

Though it was difficult, it was my decision to live with my godmother. My younger sister, who currently lives with me, is fifteen and I can't imagine her at thirteen saying she doesn't want to live with me anymore. It seems unreal that at the age of thirteen I told my biological mom I didn't want to live with her anymore.

It's sad to say, but a lot of good came out of my decision. Some of the good is I went into a stable home, excelled academically and was told every day I could do something and be somebody.

The benefit to my godmother was peace of mind. As I grew older, there were things she shared that I didn't know as a child. I'm so thankful for her because living with my biological mom made me grow up too fast and not in a good way. I knew too much at an early age. Everything was told and exposed to me. I saw so much. On the flip side, when I came to stay with my godmother on weekends and visit with her, I didn't know anything that was going on. I was like a child and it was refreshing.

I learned she had gone through custody battles, was going back and forth to court for my wellbeing. She tried to make my life better. No matter how much she wanted to keep me, she couldn't. So once I told my mom I didn't' want to live with her anymore, my godmother was able to have peace of mind. Although it was difficult, she found peace of mind once I was in a safe place and exposed to a better life. I know that made a difference.

My godmother was really brave and I now call her mom. To this day, I don't know all that went on, which I appreciate the fact she didn't tell me. Though it was a long process, it all worked out for the better. She is proud of me and I'm thankful and grateful to make her proud. I've completed high school, graduated college and have followed her teachings. She raised me in church and as she says, she's happy I'm not a hoodlum.

Unfortunately, my godmother was not successful in adopting me. I graduated with a master's in social work, partly because I want to understand the requirements and processes. I enrolled in college as an independent, because there was no joint custody. I wasn't living with my biological mother and my godmother didn't have legal power of attorney. Thankfully, I went to a private school, though I don't know if she registered me as a homeless student or what. I do know there was an agreement, because I told my mom not to try to see me and I'm sure it was tough for her as well. No mother wants to hear they didn't do well in raising their child. Therefore, I believe my godmother came to a place of being content, while my biological mom still struggles.

Influence Over Your Siblings

With my younger sister living with me, I'm hopefully giving her a better life. It's a big responsibility, but I'm so happy to have her. I have four biological siblings. I'm the oldest, then there are three brothers and my sister. One of the three brothers graduated from high school, but the other two are not living productive lives. She's the last gleam of hope to have three out of five, which are rather good statistics, to graduate from high school.

Education made the difference in my life and I'm choosing to make sure it continues. It didn't start and stop with me; it's something that will continue to change my family for generations to come. I know it's a big responsibility, but it's a responsibility I believe I have to assume.

I didn't have any influence over my one brother who did graduate from high school. When I left my biological mother, it was as if I had moved to a different country. I didn't have much interaction with them once I moved in with my godmother.

I am influencing my sister though. She attends a traditional public school in the District of Columbia. I'm happy with the decision for the moment. However, I do want to find her a different school because she's behind three grades, which is similar to my story. She's smart, but she has some academic needs. Some of the things that happened to me in the public school system are happening to her. She's at an age where she's in a lower grade than she should be. They'll push her along by putting her in the correct grade for her age, so she's not eighteen in a classroom full of younger students. I'd rather pull her out and put her in a school where she's able to master skills. When she's twenty years old nobody is going to care if she's behind three grades, but they are going to care if she can't read.

Changes You Would Contemplate
I am bias; just a little bit; just a tad; but I do think its competition. We have an education system where funding goes to public schools. I think it should be opened up, where everybody should get a piece of the pie if you are educating children. It should be an equal playing field for all schools. All entities educating children should spark more innovation. School Choice! Education Choice! Education Freedom! However you want to say it or whatever you want to call it. Creating opportunities is key.

U.S. Department of Education
Regarding influence or impact in my current position is a gray area because I'm doing this interview in my personal capacity, but I'm an advocate in my professional capacity too. Working in the department is helpful to be able to impact people's lives, share their stories and help educate people. I work in the Office of Communications and Outreach. Being able to help people understand what the Secretary's priorities are is a real treasure. There are still a lot of people who don't really understand what choice is about. There are many people in the field who have been around a long time trying to educate people on what education choice is about. What I do is capture stories, collect them and frame them in a way

people can understand what we're actually talking about. Much like what you're doing.

I believe that makes a big impact. When people understand and can put a face to the policy. When they can put a face to all the clutter out there, they're able to relate. When people see someone they know, like John across the street, it becomes more personal. That comes through by constantly telling people over and over and over again. That's what my job is, to continuously tell people stories and by sharing my story. Through sharing other people's stories; it's making a difference.

Closing Remarks
Nothing in particular, but I think what you are doing is really good.

A Few Observations:
Many of you may remember Denisha when she sat in the balcony as newly elected President Trump addressed the U.S. Congress in February 2017. Some say she has become a poster child for school choice and how allowing differing education environments can make a difference in many children's lives.

Denisha's story is one of trials and tribulations, but mostly a story of hope. She is an individual who has risen out of poverty, based partly on education opportunities and choices the state of Florida affords many of its citizens. For me, it paints a picture where she began as a dim light in a cloudy, dark sky to become a bright, shining light in that sky. The light has afforded Denisha with many events, experiences and opportunities to shine. She brings that shining offer of hope to so many.

Though her story is not unique from the perspective of being a minority inner-city child attending a failing public school, she is unique from the perspective of what this young lady has accomplished. She graduated high school from Esprit de Corps, received her undergraduate degree from the University of West Florida and will graduate with her master's degree in social work from the University of South Florida. She is the first in her immediate family to realize these accomplishments.

In addition to her academic successes, she has been afforded numerous opportunities to share her story. Doors have been opened for her to speak in various forums and capacities to include testifying before the U.S. Congress on education. As she stated above, she currently works at the U.S. Department of Education where she helps others learn about the value of a quality education and the various options there are in the states around the nation.

I agree that competition can make a big difference in education. However, the mindset must change. There are many opponents to education choice and I believe the primary reason for this is the desire to keep the status quo. Too many do not want to stop the gravy train they are riding. Remember, education is a multi-billion dollar industry. Not only are tax dollars funneled to state run schools, but all those who provide curriculum, automated systems, equipment, various support services, etc. do not want to rock the boat.

Though I am not able to relate, I am aware there are many across our nation who can relate to this story. They are living a similar life to what Denisha was born into and experienced. Anyone who watches the news will understand how desperate parents are when it comes to underperforming schools that are failing so many children.

I also have to say I was amazed at the maturity of this young lady and what she has accomplished to date. Her choice to help her younger sister shows the integrity and hope she tries to share with others on a daily basis.

Recommendations:

For those who follow education, there are many alternatives to public school. We live in a capitalist economy that rewards entrepreneurial endeavors. Though some will argue education is different, I will argue education is no different to any other business venture. We must be willing to think outside the traditional public school model. There are many options to choose from in many states. I believe it is more an issue of having the political will to change.

Solutions include charter schools, district transfers, scholarship programs, education savings accounts, private schools, homeschool and more. A one-size-fits-all model is failing too many children. Parents need to be afforded opportunities to help their children receive the best education environment that suits their needs. Parents *must* take control of their child's education.

Become an informed consumer and seek out an option to best meet your family needs. I believe all children can learn given the right environment that meets individual talents and interests. Check out your state's Department of Education website and see what options are available. Network by talking to other parents to see what they are doing and would recommend. Most of all don't settle for the status quo, as this doesn't help the child, our culture or the future of our nation. We need that entrepreneurial spirit to thrive.

Concluding Notes:

The Constitution of the State of Florida was revised in 1968 and subsequently amended. Article IX – Education consists of 8 Sections, which provides the foundation. Additional policy is found under Florida statute Title XLVIII – K-20 Education Code, Chapters 1000-1013. The document is located at http://flsenate.gov/Laws/Constitution.

The Florida Department of Education has a consumer friendly website compared to many other states. It is very clear what they offer in regards to K-12 education. You will find "School Choice" under K-12 Public Schools. The website is http://www.fldoe.org.

When it comes to education choice Florida has many options. As with most options, there are qualifying requirements and conditions to make application. The state offers Charter Schools, seven scholarship programs, virtual education, a directory for private schools as well as other choice options.

The non-profit *Step Up for Students* in Florida helps parents navigate five scholarships the state offers. This organization offers assistance through identifying the best program for a child or finding other statewide and local resources based on learning needs. The website is https://www.stepupforstudents.org.

Many organizations help parents find the right education environment for their child. National School Choice Week, a non-profit located in Santa Rosa Beach, is one organization. They work with entities around the nation to promote school choice and bring awareness to the various options parents have. Their website is https://schoolchoiceweek.com.

Sarah

Classical Conversations Curriculum

Why would a single mother consider homeschooling her only child? Sarah has a Master's degree in education, but this is no guarantee she knows how to homeschool or is a good teacher. She took the plunge anyway and began homeschooling her son because of her concern about the quality of education in public school. It wasn't always easy, money was in short supply at times and help wasn't always available. However, it is the choice and sacrifice she gladly made to ensure her son experiences what she has determined to be the best education environment for him.

Finding a New Path

I finished my degree at the University of Massachusetts while working for UMass in the CTEP program, a one-year teacher prep program. The work consisted of supervising student teachers in schools, working on the administrative side, attending faculty meetings and interacting with incoming students. I had been teaching in a Christian school in Philadelphia. Knowing I wanted to achieve getting a Masters in Education, my perspective began to change once my son was born. Having a child brings about change in many ways.

While at UMass, I worked with different students, visited schools and became more and more concerned about what I was seeing. Some teachers utilized class time as a soapbox for their political views. Others put themselves on the same level as the students. For example, if the class was playing a game where everybody's name was in a box, a student pulls out the name *Jane*, who is the teacher. I wasn't comfortable with what I was observing and knew I didn't want my son growing up in that environment. It didn't sit well. I want his academics to be strong and show respect for authority.

At UMass, I interviewed students with alternative life styles that were in opposition to our Biblical worldview. One of my concerns is that my son and I read the Bible; believe it as truth and then he would be taught the opposite at school. I didn't want him to be confused from day one. Children love and respect their teachers, so I began pursuing an understanding of classical education. Initially, homeschooling wasn't on my radar.

There was a very small classical school close to us, though I wasn't familiar with the model. I utilized my study at UMass to explore and gain understanding. I visited the school and based on a challenge to write the pre-K curriculum, I proposed it to the principal and at the end of the year was asked to be the teacher. This is how I ended up in this classical school. The first year I taught pre-K and kindergarten. We had two students, the head master's daughter and my son. Though I didn't realize it at the time, this is similar to homeschooling.

The second year, we had four students in kindergarten, 1st and 2nd grade. Again, much like homeschooling because it was four very different children. The economy began to suffer, which led to the school closing. Also, the school was in one of the poorest counties in Massachusetts. There was a lack of understanding and investment in the classical model, as well as the classical Christian education model.

Once the school closed, several of us met to consider our options. That was when I began to consider homeschooling. As a single mother, I thought it would be impossible, but through a series of events and the way God provided for us financially, it became possible.

The first year was when my son was in 1st grade and some of us met a few days a week. This arrangement concerned me, because I didn't feel I had accountability. I needed structure; a plan. My love of designing curriculum fueled my need to make sure I had accountability and was going in the right direction. This drove me to seek out a structured option. I came across *Classical Conversations* and started the first group in Massachusetts over a decade ago.

Limited Options

My options seemed limited at UMass. Based on what I saw from potential and current educators, I knew public school was not the right environment for my son. My perception was not everyone is able to homeschool, yet everyone should have access to high quality education. Parents who are not able to send their child to a private school or homeschool should also expect quality education. This is interesting because public schools believe they have the best education and alternatives are subpar, but this is my opinion.

When the classical school closed and I began to consider homeschooling, there really weren't other viable options. I briefly wondered if I could work in one of the private schools in the area and have my son attend, but this wasn't the best option for us at the time. Private schools were expensive, difficult to get into and had a different education philosophy. The closest Christian school was over an hour away, so realistically there were limited options.

Multiple Factors Considered

First was my dissatisfaction with what was happening in public schools.

The second factor is my love of the classical model. It was designed in a way we are best able to learn. I wanted to continue learning and knew it was how my son should be educated. Bottom line is homeschooling was a viable option and there weren't any classical schools in this part of Massachusetts. There might have been one or two near Boston, but the philosophy I wanted to pursue was a primary factor.

Third, my thought was I'm a teacher and I don't teach my own son. This seemed somewhat silly.

The last factor speaks more to location. The western side of the state along the I91 corridor, has five colleges in the area, is rural and it's forty-five minutes to the closest city. It's probably the most liberal area in MA, but ironically was where Jonathan Edwards first evangelized and traveled. Today the area takes pride in being progressive and leads in what society considers *forward thinking*.

Classical Conversations Program

The Classical Conversations community is twenty minutes from where we live and some students travel two and a half hours each way to participate. There are a couple of students who travel Monday, stay the night, attend class the next day and drive home after class. Of the thirteen students in my class, only four or five live less than forty-five minutes from the facility we meet in. Due to the limited options, parents must travel if they want their child to participate in the program and many do.

I wanted to continue with this education philosophy and it connects with my need for accountability. We tend to teach to our strengths, so my concern with just homeschooling is I would always teach to my strengths. What about the other areas my son needs to learn that I'm not as strong in? He might not have learned as much about geography if not for Classical Conversations, as this is not my strength. When he did Challenge A, the 7th grade program, he learned how to map the world and many of the students doing it from memory, which is remarkable.

Another positive is when your child gets older the program provides more curriculum. Younger children begin with a skeletal program, which I equate to the backbone of a body. Parents are able to fill in the curriculum with whatever they believe is important. Older children are provided a full syllabus for each year the student attends and parents can tailor it as they see fit. It's nice for parents to look at the scope and sequence for 7th through 12th grades, know what their child will receive and graduate with more credits then required.

Classical Conversations is an academically rigorous program, but parents have the freedom to tailor it for their child. If a child wants to travel or play sports or whatever, they can tailor the program as needed. Or, maybe a child is struggling academically. For example, one student in my class was reading below grade level, yet he had a great mind and was a deep thinker. He could engage in the dialog and discussions, so at home he might listen to audio books or things to help him with content until he improves his reading.

Biggest Hurdle

Homeschooling can be a hurdle or challenge for a single mom. For me, it was a financial question as to how I would provide for my son if I were to homeschool instead of work fulltime. I don't receive child support or help like that. This was the biggest hurdle.

A smaller hurdle was books and other supplies, but people have loaned us books or we buy used. There are states, like California, that offer umbrella programs for homeschoolers. They also pay for other programs and provide various types of support. Unfortunately, Massachusetts provides no support for homeschoolers.

Though not a big hurdle, there are reporting requirements. Parents are required to report in the fall, mid-year and at the end of the school year. I personally haven't had any problems with this; simply submit what's required and nothing more or less. I submit a letter stating my son's course of study for the year, including specific curricular choices for each subject area. About a month later, I receive an approval letter.

Depending on the district, some parents will be instructed to provide something like the amount of time the child will be in school or other specifics that are not required.

For those who do have problems, Home School Legal Defense Association or HSLDA is a parent's biggest advocate. They are a group of lawyers who provide legal defense and parents can obtain membership in the organization. Typically, HSLDA is contacted when a parent submits the required paperwork at the beginning of the year to homeschool and are asked to submit additional information. This is when parents send in the HSLDA form showing what they're required to provide. Usually, the district accepts this once they see HSLDA is involved.

As a taxpayer, it's frustrating the schools don't help much. Some homeschoolers have had positive experiences with the high school playing sports. However, things like speaking with a guidance counselor or an academic advisor to discuss college is not supported. A friend and I have called and were told public school doesn't provide services to homeschoolers, which as taxpayers is not right.

Though the biggest hurdle is financial, I am grateful to God who made it possible for me to work for Classical Conversations. I'm the Area Representative for the program in Massachusetts and Rhode Island, but also tutor a class one day a week for the 10th and 11th graders in Challenge 2.

Playing Sports

The school district does allow homeschooled children to participate in high school sports. One of our Classical Conversation graduates ran track, had a brother who played basketball and another brother played baseball. There is a young lady who lives in another school district and participates in Nordic skiing. Playing sports doesn't seem to be an issue for homeschoolers.

Because my son hasn't been involved in sports, I'm not aware of any issues regarding athletics. We haven't pursued this opportunity due to distance, costs associated with participating and the need to be at the school every day at 2:30pm. There are other options and my son does Tae Kwon Do year around, snowboards, runs, bikes and so I'm not concerned. As a younger child, he participated in rec leagues, which are less expensive, but once a child turns twelve the option is to play for the high school.

Greatest Challenge to Overcome
Being a single mother and struggling financially is the greatest challenge. The truth is God has always provided, but it's not always been easy. I chose not to pursue my career, even though I have a master's degree. Not because I'm a hero or anything like that, but because I believe my son's soul comes first; then his academics. I'll have time once he's in college to pursue other things.

Teaching your own child is sometimes a blessing and sometimes not, because it can be difficult. He's the student I love the most, but he's also the student that gives me the most trouble. I believe it's because we live together and there's the challenge of knowing when to wear my teacher hat or my mom hat. Also, I'm dealing with the finances, taking care of the yard (though he does a lot of that now) and helping my elderly parents who live next door. Trying to manage everything and homeschool has its challenges, but I don't regret it at all.

When I was considering homeschooling after the classical school closed, I met a homeschool mother of six who had been widowed. She challenged me to homeschool even though she probably didn't even look at it as a challenge. She told me it would be the most humbling thing I will have ever done. That is certainly the case.

Benefits Realized
The freedom my son has to do part-time jobs or different things and the ability to make his own schedule. We get to spend a lot of time together, so I get to know the way my son

thinks. I know where he's struggling and where his strengths are.

I chose the classical model of deep discussions, inference, developing wisdom and virtue. I believe he's on track because I see in him deep thought and a growing integrity. If he was away every day and came home in the evenings, I believe I would be harping on him to get his work done. I don't believe we'd have our deep discussions. I'd say these are some of the ways both of us have benefited.

What Would You Change
Regarding schools in Massachusetts, a lot of what I said earlier regarding soapboxes and using school as a platform to espouse political views. I don't believe it's the responsibility of a teacher to tell students the government is wrong. The priority should be teaching children how to read, write, do math, and to think clearly and logically.

Final Word
As I stated up front, homeschooling is not for everybody and many cannot afford Christian or private school. The education system should provide a standard across the board so everybody gets a quality education, even a Classical education. I recognize this is a very tall order.

I believe as more people pull out of the public school system to explore other options, it will cause people to rethink what is being done and consider changing the current system. As more individuals pursue a classical education with the understanding they are teaching children how to think and to reason, I believe society will realize much stronger thinkers in the future. That is my prayer anyway.

A Few Thoughts:

There are a few things I find compelling about Sarah's story. The first being Sarah is an educator. I would say the majority of teachers believe public education is the best environment for children. The second point is she lives in Massachusetts where I presumed education options would be more abundant. With bastions of academic thought and creativity that include Cambridge, Harvard and MIT, I have to admit I was surprised to learn K-12 options are fairly limited.

All fifty states have options, which fall under one of the following: public, private or homeschool. Massachusetts does offer options, but are limited and fall within the public school system. The state claims to offer the best and most sought after higher education institutions in the world, so why not the best and most sought after choices when it comes to K-12 education?

I agree being a single mother has its challenges when it comes to homeschooling. Parents must be willing to make sacrifices if they choose this option. But, where there is a will – there is a way. Within the past decade many organizations and groups have formed specifically to support homeschool families.

Homeschool is the fastest growing option in the U.S. and there are a multitude of reasons for the growth. One reason is it can be the least out-of-pocket costs to the parents. There are minimal expenses such as curriculum, supplies, possibly technology or subject specific items. However, based on my knowledge and experience, there are two primary drivers for this choice: bullying/safety concerns and social conditioning. Public school tries to accommodate for every issue for everyone. Like Sarah, many parents want their child educated based on a foundational belief system.

As reported by the U.S. Department of Education, National Center for Education Statistics (NCES) in 2016 there were 3.3 percent or 1,690,000 children participating in homeschool. More current data reflects a 3.4 to 3.5 percent or 2,000,000 plus children homeschooled.

There are pros and cons to everything in life. As the parent it is up to you to do the analysis and decide if the pros outweigh the cons. The analysis and decision will ultimately make it clear as to what is the best education environment for your child.

Recommendations:

The first thing to understand if you are inclined to homeschool your child is: *you can do this.* Too many parents are talked out of homeschooling for various reasons with the number one being fear, of not being educated enough to homeschool. Nonsense! There are so many resources and groups out there for emotional support as well as coursework, field trips, testing, etc.

Homeschool is an education option that does receive negative pressure from teachers unions and public education institutions. There are organizations in the business of helping parents know their rights and navigate the application process. As Sarah mentioned, a national organization to be familiar with is the Home School Legal Defense Association (HSLDA). They are in the business of protecting the legal rights of parents who choose to homeschool. I would recommend visiting their website and familiarize yourself with your parental rights.

Know what your state has legislated regarding homeschooling. Each state's Department of Education has language based on legislation to let parents know what is required and must be complied with. Don't rely solely on what the school district says or provides. Remember, public schools receive funding based on the number of students enrolled. Be an informed consumer.

Concluding Notes:

Massachusetts asserts to have the world's oldest functioning written constitution. The 1780 Constitution of the Commonwealth of Massachusetts was written by John Adams and speaks of education in *Part the Second, Chapter V.* Stemming from the constitution is the Massachusetts General Law (MGL) where education can be found in Part 1, Article XII, Chapters 69-78A.

The Massachusetts Department of Education (DOE) identifies the state offers public school to include charters, inter-district and virtual; private or parochial school; and homeschool. A list of public, private or parochial schools for parents to decide what is a viable option can be found at http://www.doe.mass.edu/SchProgramOptions.html.

All states allow some form of homeschooling as an option with each state identifying the criteria and reporting elements involved. The Massachusetts DOE does not readily identify homeschooling, but it does identify this as an option under "School & Program Options." Parents are instructed to contact their local superintendent's office for information when they choose to homeschool.

Classical Conversations, the homeschool curriculum Sarah advocates, provides information, resources and support at https://www.classicalconversations.com. You can easily find a *Community Support Representative* in your state as well as some overseas locations should you determine this program a good fit for your child.

One last source to mention is the Home School Legal Defense Association (HSLDA). This organization has a membership option and provides legal support for homeschool families. Non-members can view https://hslda.org for various resources.

Gina

Public School Math Teacher Becomes Private Math Tutor

Everybody loves math – right? Gina loves math and teaching math. It's an easy subject when you know and follow the rules. Everyone can do math if they understand the logic and process regarding calculations and formulas. At least that is what she believes.

In the Beginning
I didn't start out as a math teacher. My degree is in accounting and was a CPA for several years, but found no fulfillment from that career. Though I made good money, this is not what drives me. I have a need to change the world one little person at a time, because that's who I am. So I shifted gears, took the required classes to become a high school math teacher and loved it. I loved the relationships with the children, teaching the math and seeing light bulbs go on. It was like that for a long time.

The Road Turned
Once I had children I stepped away for a few years, but came back. I took another break for a few years when my daughter was sick, then returned to the classroom. This stepping away

and coming back is when I really noticed the changes. The class I was teaching was pre-calculus or math analysis, which I could no longer teach. Not so much that the children weren't able to learn, but more that they were not equipped with the basic skills. Towards the end of my teaching career, I was required to provide calculation assignments during the summer to be done by hand, such as 24 x 86. Some children going into pre-calculus could not do that.

Due to standardized testing, the focus shifted to passing a test. This focus is living in the moment, not preparing for the future. It's about teachers ensuring students' get the grade right now, so let's teach students how to use a calculator. Starting as early as 6th grade children are given a calculator. In theory, they learned how to do fractions, percent and basic multiplying by hand, but they never had to do it again. Our muscles will atrophy if we don't use them and the same goes for our minds.

Using a calculator is very frustrating as children come in and can't do anything. I reaped the detriments from that when I was teaching. Though it was frustrating, I continued to press on because I still enjoyed the children. I was not known as the easy teacher, in part because I would give tests where calculators could only be used for certain problems. My goal was to encourage them to understand math, the foundational parts they lost and to do math.

Then came the straw that broke the camel's back. In my last year, I taught pre-calculus and a geometry class. Some high school students taking geometry are not the brightest, but it's okay. Everyone isn't great in math and that's expected. During the first semester, I taught them well, the way I wanted to teach them. Going into the second semester, many students from across the school failed geometry part one.

The administration decided to have a repeat class for the students who failed. Nobody wanted to teach the class, so I thought I'd teach the class. This class consisted of the students who had all failed, some because of attendance or discipline and some because they didn't get math or weren't good at math.

Originally, I was told to teach this class and reteach geometry part one. However, the schedule was changed. I was expected to teach the repeat class of thirty students and geometry parts one and two for the semester. In addition, they all needed to pass the SOLs in May. I looked at who these students were, concluded they were having a difficult time and probably weren't ever going to use the geometry or didn't care.

For good or bad I'm embarrassed to say, I decided I was going to get them to pass the test, so I taught to the test. The students hated me, which I'm not used to. I was forcing math into them and when it was SOL time, the majority passed. The administration was expecting all in the class to fail. By this time the students loved me because I gave them something they wanted; pass the SOL. The administration loved it and gave me kudos. However, I made it clear I didn't teach math, I taught the students how to pass a test.

Without consulting me, the administration made what I consider an unpopular decision. The second to the last day of the school year, I was told I was clearly gifted at teaching students geometry. Since I hadn't been consulted, I asked if the pre-calculus students were consulted because I believe they will say I'm clearly gifted at teaching pre-calculus. The administration stated we need you to teach geometry, so your schedule for next year will be to teach geometry, the lowest end geometry, because this is where you are gifted. In addition, we want you to teach the other geometry teachers how to do what you did.

They wanted me to teach all the math teachers how to not teach math, because I didn't teach math. I taught students how to pass a test. I was asked to not teach geometry to students, not help them in their future endeavors, but simply help the schools statistics.

I'm sure it was assumed, because I'm a non-married woman and counting on myself, that I was going to agree. I don't know if that is true or not, but that was my thought. The next day, the last day of school, I removed all my belongings when I left at the end of the day. I wanted to decide over the summer what I would do.

Since I was a twelve-month employee, having a paycheck was not a concern. Every day I asked myself if this is what I want to do. I had left an accounting job to do something I love, because doing something that matters in the world makes a difference. I didn't want to do something I thought might be hurting these students.

I went to the school three weeks later to let the administration know if this is where they want to go, then they will have to go without me. This is not what I want to be a part of. I wasn't even concerned about being offered my previous position back, because the same thing would happen the following year. I knew I would be without a job, didn't have a plan, but I would be paid to the end of the summer. I gave them my official notice, but the principal wanted to talk. I knew he was doing what he thought was best for the school, but I need to do what is best for me. I wanted us all to leave this situation on good terms, so I walked away and that was it.

This was when the road turned, when they told me in their own words not to teach math.

Important To Love What You Do

I was expected to do something I did not love, did not believe in and thought would be detrimental. This solidified my decision. It's important to love what you do and to have a job that doesn't hurt others. I knew I would hurt the future of every student who did not learn geometry in my class. In addition, I wouldn't be able to teach the upper level students, which was really my gift.

I've felt this way before, when there are good teachers being taken advantage of and it's a frustrating truth. I'm a good teacher. It's not okay to be treated this way. I believe I was being punished for being good.

Impact of Technology

Technology is a massive impact. The year came when all math classrooms were getting smart boards. This was funny because I prefer having a lot of whiteboard space so students can get up and do their own work. While in the classroom, a person came in to let me know a smart board was going to be installed. I expressed that I simply wanted whiteboards and asked if I had to have one. The person responded with a yes and asked where would I like the board placed.

This particular room had a view of the courtyard where students go for lunch and can be very distracting, so I asked the smart board be put opposite the courtyard. There was some debate, but I finally looked at the person and said if the smart board is for the children, then put it where I said.

One of the things I loved about whiteboards is to have them across the whole front of the class. We would work a problem, talk it through, leave the problem there and go to the next board to work the next problem. When students grappled with something about the first problem, they could look at it and have time to figure it out. When we finished the second problem, and only then, I would erase the first problem. This allowed the students to see all the calculations. A smart board doesn't allow students to see all of one problem, particularly when doing math analysis, which these problems can be quite lengthy.

There are times when smart boards just don't work, at least where we put them. It may be a cost savings, but the smart board is put over the whiteboard, which was put over the chalkboard. The whiteboard isn't even an option because the whiteboard has been covered up.

My perfect classroom would consist of whiteboards all the way around with plenty of markers. Students, in pairs so they can help each other, would get up, do the problems and I could see where they are going wrong. This gets them out of their seats and doing something other than sitting there like they're on an assembly line. Also, we're doing the same thing for everybody.

Yes, I'm very anti-smart board. I used it as a glorified whiteboard, because I thought that's all it was. To me it was a waste of money and space and detrimental to the students.

Let's talk calculators; I believe they've been a big problem and I'm about to give away my secret. We should invent a calculator that will not do operations between one and two digit numbers, specifically for schools. If a problem is 12 x 6 or 12 x 64 or 64 - 12, it won't calculate. This would force students to remember how to calculate. People who can do two digit numbers can do three and four digit numbers.

For the higher order problems and fractions give students a calculator and not waste our lives. To calculate 1/2 x 5/8, simply type into the calculator 1 divided by 2 x 5 divided by 8 and hit enter, hit enter again and it turns into a fraction. The calculator does it all. I think a calculator designed like that specifically for schools would be a great thing.

In reality, calculators have become a problem, though there is a place for them. It's not that we shouldn't have them. It's more that we shouldn't be using them the way they are being used now.

In today's age of technology, there are math apps students can get. For example, in Algebra I they use Polysmlt root finder. It basically allows students to never learn how to factor, which is a pretty major thing to learn in high school going up through Calculus and beyond. Students simply need to know how to use the app. Maybe there should be a class called *calculator operation* and don't call it math, because it's not.

Another app is Photomath, which is pretty amazing. One of my students showed me and all you have to do is hover your phone over a math problem and it will calculate the solution. Students are using this app to get answers to their homework. It's fast and also shows how the answer was calculated. Students today want solutions fast and they don't want any struggling time. We need to have some struggle in order to figure things out or we'll never get it. We'll lose the critical thinking capability. However, I admit this app is a good tool for students to use.

One thing I did regularly in the pre-calculus class was record on the smart board the lesson where students would hear my voice and see what I'm writing. I could upload these lessons for students to have access to them. It's exactly what they learned in class, but they can slow it down, rewind it and revisit what they missed. Many students said they would review these lessons for the tests.

Yes, technology can be helpful, but too many times it's a distraction such as phones in the classroom. It can be discouraging and I still believe technology has done far more bad then good things.

Overall Objective for Tutoring
One of the objectives is to improve the lack of confidence derived from students not knowing the basics. I want students to truly do math, so they can feel confident in what they're doing. Without confidence we'll create a generation of people who can't do anything. On a macro level, I want my students to come in, learn math and feel they can go on and be successful. To learn something now that lasts.

For instance, students would say they want to use their calculator on a test and I would tell them no. This teaches them to go back and learn the things that are not hard to learn. They are forced to learn for one hour a week. They need to be able to use their math later; in classes, in life, and give change to somebody at the store. They need to figure out a discount or if they can afford to buy something. That's my objective.

Several Benefits to Tutoring
Deciding to tutor was a big jump and, quite honestly, I wasn't sure I could make it. I asked a friend of mine who tutors for a living if she thought I could. Remember, I don't have a husband to take care of me financially. This friend had no

reservations and really encouraged me. I started in February, which isn't necessarily the best time to begin as most students already have their tutors. Fortunately, I filled up within about one and a half months. Once people find out you are a math tutor, it doesn't take long, because there is such a need.

One personal and gratifying benefit is I get to see the light bulb go on. Another gift I have is figuring out where students went wrong and then I can see where their process went awry. Often I'll make students speak what they're thinking so I can understand what's going on in their heads. Sometimes they'll get the right answer and the way they got it works for this problem, but not the next. All of the sudden it's like where did I go wrong. I really enjoy this personalized aspect of being able to figure things out.

Another benefit is the students think I'm a hero. While in school teaching, I believe many students thought I was the one who could give them a bad grade. I'm not sure they looked at education as a privilege, but rather looked at it as a place they had to be with the goal of getting an "A" and didn't care much about the learning.

Students now come to me for one hour. They sit down and know what they don't know. They must arrive on time because at the end of the sixty minutes they know someone else is coming. The student comes in, has self-diagnosed what they need to be working on and we go from there, so each day is different. I know which student will arrive, but the session changes based on student needs. We all benefit because they come in and I solve their problem by helping them figure it out. The students and their parents think I'm great and I do believe I'm changing the world a little bit.

One example I'll share is a student took Algebra I in 8th grade, a little advanced, and received an "A" in the course, but failed the standardized test. One might ask how this is possible. The dad talked to me and sent him over for the summer because he was scheduled to retake the SOL. I worked with him and discovered he didn't know squat without a calculator. To figure out what -1 + -2 equals he had to use his calculator. Same thing for figuring out what 4 x 6 equates to. This child was trying to figure things out and somehow did it well enough to get an "A" in the course.

One day I said I'll never tell your dad, but asked if he had cheated. He said he didn't, that he understood the problems at the time, but wasn't able to retain the information. We worked like crazy to get the skills back and on some test taking strategies, because there was a point where the immediate goal is to pass the SOL. However, the long-term goal was you have to do Algebra I to do Geometry. The student is in Geometry, not using a calculator and doing a great job. His dad told me to plan on having him until he graduates.

I told this student he would be tempted to go back to using the calculator. Though it may take you a little bit longer to do a problem, choose to use your brain. You have the time because other people are slow on their calculators. Your brain is the best tool you have. The calculator, like any tool, doesn't have to be used every time just because you have the tool.

The kind of growth and excitement I see when a student lets me know they passed or they come in and self-diagnose what they need are immeasurable benefits. Students are obviously gaining or getting the grade they want and sometimes less frustration. One of the big things going on is IXL, which has many math problems. In theory, it's a great idea. It will take a very narrow topic like multiplying exponents and give you a lot of problems. It's computer based, it gives a question and if the student gets it right they get points. If they get it wrong, it takes away points.

One thing happening is teachers will forgo traditional homework and handwriting and only use IXL. It's frustrating because students need to get at least eighty percent for it to count as completed homework and some students don't know how to use IXL. They lose points and don't have anybody to help them. I gave one student an IXL assignment and asked her why she didn't do the assignment. Her response was she already had an anger issue and using IXL makes it worse.

I realize IXL is frustrating, but one of the advantages is I want them to love math, not hate it. They arrive for their appointment and are still doing the work. I don't simply help them select an answer, we work on what's wrong so they score at least an eighty percent and we move on. There is some value in IXL, even though it is frustrating for them. This is another benefit student's get from me.

Another example is just this morning a student sent me a text and is taking a pre-calculus class at one of the private schools. She took a photo of the board that listed what was going to be on their next test. I looked at it, wrote her back and said I'm concerned about numbers one and three. She's been working on number one and thinks she's okay. I'm not sure any of the homework we've looked at covers number three, which she knows and is not sure what to do about it, so I texted her some of those types of questions with solutions. The students know even though they are not coming to see me at the moment, I'm nerdy, love math and will do things like this. I'll take a picture and send it back to them. The students do this regularly.

The biggest benefit to the students is overall confidence. I have a 5th grade student who is one of triplets. When he first started, you knew he was thinking, but seemed almost afraid to answer the question for fear of messing up. One day he said he couldn't believe I was ever a teacher in a school, because I was nice. He had this thought that all teachers or maybe just math teachers were mean. I tell him that if he wasn't messing up, he wasn't trying hard enough. If I don't want you to mess up, I'll ask you what 1+1 equals all the time. If I'm not challenging you, then there's no point. He needed to hear it was okay to mess up, because when you mess up, you're learning.

I've been working with this student for about a semester and he's a different child. He comes skipping in and his mother says he loves coming in and doing the math. He has confidence and I believe this experience changed the way he views school. He needed to hear teachers are not mad with him. I've gotten as much out of this as he has and I really believe this is a huge thing for him.

The traffic from my bedroom to where I tutor is never bad and I dress however I want. Sometimes, like this morning, I'll have a student at 7:30am because students will come in before school. I went to the gym beforehand so I had a ponytail and dried on sweat, but the student didn't care. I love it.

I recently had an unexpected expense. I had to expand my driveway because one student would park in the driveway and the next student would tear up my front lawn. The front lawn got so bad I had to do something. Never thought I'd need a wider driveway, but then I had to teach these sixteen year olds how to park in the driveway.

The last benefit is I earn more money than I did in the public school system. Though it's not about the money, it's nice to know I can pay my bills. I make my own schedule, which sometimes is a little too full. One of the things I need to work on is how to say *no*. Recently, I finished my first full year of tutoring and was concerned about making it work, so I said *yes* all the time. While I do have flexibility with my schedule and time, I tend to fill it up.

Hurdles to Overcome
Initially, I worried I wouldn't succeed. I had to figure out how I was going to pay for health insurance, because that can be quite costly.

It was never a problem getting students. Initially, my friend who tutors would send me her overflows and several students were glad I began tutoring. It's important to send students to someone who is good, so I began through referrals. Now I'm referring my overflow to another friend who began tutoring.

Ensuring the S-corporation paperwork was completed and filed. Given my CPA background I knew what to do, but not necessarily what all needed to be filed. I enlisted the expertise of someone else to help me complete this process. The business elements needed to be dealt with, but it was an easy transition from public school to private math tutor.

Another big hurdle is how to fit eating into my schedule, because it's difficult to eat while tutoring. I've learned to have my biggest meal of the day at lunchtime, because dinner is when many of my students are free. I work from 2pm until 8pm or 9pm every day with students coming every hour, on the hour.

A hurdle I'm trying to figure out now is how to help more students. One thing I'm working on now is how to do some sort of weekly webinar by class, as weekly tutoring time. Students would pay based on a monthly fee, which will provide four one-hour webinars. I would be accessible to answer questions during the webinar, but would have to tailor the course to what a particular school is doing.

I believe I have a gift for teaching math. My mind is very simple, I think in simple ways and believe it translates well to children. So, how can I help more children?

Greatest Mind Shift to Overcome

The mind shift to recognize that working every single day makes a difference. When I don't work, I don't get paid. All of a sudden, I don't want a sick day. Not that I took them before, but I took them for granted. For example, when it's snowing outside and the students don't' have school, they can't get to my location either. These are things I really had to think about. My financial background taught me to be good with money and thinking long term. However, when I haven't worked for two weeks I notice the impact to my personal budget.

I have to rely one hundred percent on myself, not simply go to school and receive a paycheck. Even though I was relying on myself as a single parent, I have a work ethic and felt someone else had my back. Now I do this all alone. All along, I wanted to teach math and to teach children, but now I'm getting the opportunity to do this on my terms.

I tutor high school and love high school students. Then I begin tutoring middle school students because some take Geometry and Algebra I. Middle school friends find out about me and then I'm tutoring middle school students in pre-Algebra. Soon I receive calls from elementary students.

For example, I received a call regarding a 2nd grader who didn't like math, didn't feel good about it and the parent asked me to work with their daughter. I was sure I wasn't the girl for the job, because my strength is in the upper levels. However, this parent said she heard I was the girl.

We began with a trial period as I was wondering what I'm going to do with a 2nd grader. We started with half an hour instead of my typical hour and if it doesn't work, we agreed to stop the sessions. A couple of months went by and what a treasure this child is. I'm working on very different things like elapsed time, problems such as how much time is there between 9:20 and 10:35. Things she didn't understand such as how tens place and ones place were different. How the number 14 is a 10 and a 4 and why when you get 10 ones it moves into another column. This has been a great challenge for me because I'm figuring out what to do. One day I went to the bank and got a roll of quarters, dimes, nickels and pennies and dumped them out and we worked on money.

The challenge of learning how to tutor has been the greatest mind shift or benefit to me. As I mentioned, I never really know what I'm doing from one day to the next. Such a wide range where some days I'm working with a 2nd grader, followed by pre-Calculus, followed by Algebra II and end with a college calculus student. Tutoring math is all over the place and I don't have time to get bored, it just keeps going.

Changes You Would Make
Number one is let children fail, because this is a big thing. I would change the grading system, but somebody else would have to figure out how to do this. Let's say we keep the A, B, C, D and F and in every single class instead of having grades,

let's have ranks. The top twenty percent get ranked first, the next twenty percent rank second, the next twenty percent ranked third and so forth. This resembles the world where employees are graded compared to their peers. If a person excels as a salesman, it's because they are a better salesmen, not because they've been in the company longer or attended something. This could make a huge difference. Unfortunately, twenty percent in this scenario fail every class, but it would raise the level of everybody.

The calculator change mentioned earlier. I'm speaking specifically about math and changing the calculator so it can't do one and two digit operations.

Students feel entitled to school and believe it's a gift they can have, not have or don't really care. This needs to change, so I would give every single student in every school a job at the school to ensure every student has ownership in the school. If students were in charge of emptying the trash, there would be fewer custodial employees. Have students clean up the lunchroom and students on the baseball team maintain the grass on the ball field. Students should have ownership, which will cause a shift in jobs because somebody has to monitor the students to ensure things are done. I'm just an idea person, but something like this has to happen where the students understand they are paying for their education. When things are free, there is no realized value. If things have to be paid for, people will recognize the value.

There are a lot of students and families who use school as a babysitter, until age eighteen, which is not essential. Let's keep high school in high school and college in college. It's not necessary to have all the AP classes in high school when students can do them in college. Let's teach the basics in high school, but at age sixteen or 10th grade they finish. Students could test into 11th or 12th grade, but it's not a given. That way the students who really don't care can move on with life. By 10th grade students have learned what they need to learn or what they are going to learn. Send the sixteen year olds to get a job, maybe at entry level, but people need to learn work ethic and job skills. They need to show up to work on time and learn customer service skills. This may not be a popular thought, but that's what I think.

Summers off have been a real detriment to students, at least for math. It supports doing a brain dump on everything and starting fresh in the next school year. The truth is at the high school level there is prerequisite knowledge students must have. Passing a test may not be a problem, but over the summer, not using it is. I would prefer having more breaks rather than having the whole summer off.

Closing Remarks

The one thing I want to try to figure out is my business plan and how to help more students. I really don't care if I earn more money. At times, I would like to work a few less hours, but my main focus is to help students be successful in math.

My three plus four cents:

Math is a subject where many people, not just Gina's students, struggle. Whether you are in elementary school, a cashier in a retail business or someone balancing your checkbook, too many people will say they aren't good at math.

Many of us have heard over the years, a teacher's primary reason for leaving the field of education is because the pay is too low. That may be part of the decision for some, but I've concluded there are many other reasons. I've decided teachers will accept the pay if they believe they have respect, flexibility, are supported and know they are helping students succeed. For many, their love and passion of teaching outweigh the financial compensation.

I would argue math doesn't have to be as complicated as many believe it to be. There was a time when I loved math. I found it challenging and I loved working Pythagorean theorem problems. Over the years, I've developed an opinion where I believe it's more about the way math is taught, not the student trying to learn, that is the real culprit.

While attending an education seminar I watched a video where a math teacher was giving a lesson on calculating circumference and angles. There was some instruction, then students worked in pair's, then additional instruction, then students worked in groups, and then the teacher brought it all together by relating the calculated measurements to a satellite dish. This manner of instruction allowed the students to hear, do and see how these calculations relate to their daily lives. They understand that without a satellite dish, they will not have TV reception. Without a communication satellite, they will not have cell phone service. Engage students and they will learn.

I was inspired by Gina's passion when she was sharing the many stories about starting her tutoring business and the range of students she has helped and continues to help. She brings enthusiasm to what many refer to as a dreaded subject: *math*. Her candor, willingness and common sense were refreshing.

I would venture to say another benefit she is realizing is she no longer has to consider or worry about retaliation from the administration. I'm not surprised to hear of the situation that led to her decision to leave the public education system. I agree good teachers do get used and abused and are expected to pick up the slack in any given department. Now she is her own boss and sets her own schedule.

Deciding to start a tutoring business, as a single woman, can be an extremely risky adventure. Leaving the security of a steady paying job to transition into an unknown financial opportunity would make many people think twice or maybe three times before taking the leap. However, Gina was confident in what she wanted to do, had help from friends and came to realize she had the right attitude and skills to succeed. She has proven it was the right decision for her.

Recommendations:

Don't struggle with math. It truly is a set of rules for calculating numbers and letters and doesn't have to be as difficult as many make it out to be.

If you do struggle with math, seek out individuals like Gina or speak to your child's school to determine what resources are available in your area. There are many resources to tap into and some are provided at no cost.

Never let math be a factor that prohibits you from moving forward with aspirations and achieving goals. There are many tools to help individuals understand the basics of math and more. Technology, for better or worse, has changed the way people learn.

Most of all, apply yourself. Learn what you need to learn to be successful in whatever career or venture you choose. Hard work, a positive attitude and a good work ethic pays great dividends and *your* success is dependent on *your* efforts to succeed.

Concluding Notes:

Some states have well developed Department of Education websites that provide a range of resources for parents and students. A search on the website may provide some useful information. However, be aware that states who are not education choice friendly may provide very limited or no information outside of the public school system.

There are many resources in many communities that help with tutoring. Make inquiries as to whether there are public school teachers who do tutoring on a part-time basis. Public schools may offer possible tutoring options after school for little or no additional cost to enrolled students.

Seek out non-profits that help with struggling students in learning math. If you are not familiar with local organizations, perform an Internet search. There are social media pages where individuals can make inquiries and receive recommendations. Local civic organizations such as the Chamber of Commerce, Lions Club, AAUW and many more typically have individuals willing to help.

Lastly, you can find Gina's book titled "21 Ways to Improve Your Math Grade in 30 Days or Less" on Amazon.com.

Annie

Private School Teacher

If you think private school is expensive, you would be right in this case. Annie teaches in an affluent private school in an eastern state.

A Math Teacher's Journey

I have a love and passion for math. This is why I believe I fell into the private school sector because my degree is in engineering and mathematics. I didn't seek to earn a teaching degree or credentials, so my options were limited for teaching in the public school system. That's primarily how I fell into the private school sector.

I have extensive knowledge of math and I chose to teach math, but needed the credentials to teach in public school. I may be wrong now, but I've been teaching for many years and having certain degrees and credentials was the rule when I started. This may have changed, but I love teaching in private school and don't consider public school anymore.

What I love about teaching in a private school is the small class size and the level of rigor I'm able to hold most of my students too. There are high expectations set for the students. I primarily teach AP math courses with a set curriculum, but I have complete autonomy over my classroom from the perspective of how I get through the material, the approach I take and the order in which we proceed. I really enjoy having the flexibility and don't seem to have a lot of the red tape public school teachers have.

We have access to an endless supply of resources at our fingertips. If I need markers, I go to the supply closet and grab two boxes of markers. I'm able to make as many photocopies as I need for my class. I'm able to go on professional development trips every year. I believe there are several nice perks private school teachers enjoy.

The school is accredited through a state approved entity and a member of the National Association of Independent Schools (NAIS). This was completed after I returned from several years of teaching in a private school in a western state.

Regarding specific curriculum, as an AP teacher I'm accountable for the AP curriculum. As a math teacher and part of the math department, there's always discussion amongst the team regarding what students need to do to move to the next class and what students learned prior to. It's a smooth flow within our math department.

East vs. West

Teaching in a private school in a liberal western state versus teaching in a conservative eastern state are two very different experiences. In the west, we would spend days, meeting on end, talking about how the faculty felt about something and how the students felt about something. It was more about feelings.

For example, when we were setting a dress code we couldn't state anything that was offensive to the girls. On the other hand, we couldn't state anything that was offensive to the boys. Therefore, the dress code ended up being students had to wear clothing that would cover where undergarments should be worn.

In the east, one school started a club for students in the LGBT community. Students in my class made fun of the group. It seems they don't have any concept or are less informed of the world outside of their community. I realize this might be horrible to say, because I love the school and the students, but they have no idea of what's happening in the outside world.

In the western states it's more of a teaching style and what we were trying to do was apply more focus on the global community to consider what good we could do. The eastern states seem to focus more on grades and learning.

Pros and Cons
Yes, there are pros and cons between working in the west versus working in the east. I think the pros of working in a private school on the west coast, or at least the one I worked at, is we're raising global citizens. People, who care about other people, are conscientious of the environment, of feelings and seem to have a greater sense of awareness that the world doesn't revolve around them.

A con is feelings get hurt, so teachers need to be careful of what and how they say something to a student. It's not advisable to tell any student they didn't understand the material on the test and that's why they got an F. Reasons include maybe the test was bias or I didn't ask the question in the way they could understand. There was a lot of hand holding, never any accountability and it seemed like whenever something happened, we could find an excuse. There was a way to justify anything based from, well, where they're from. This seemed to be the way it was.

A definitive pro in the east is there are set expectations. Students take many AP courses and the expectation is the teachers will help students earn fours and fives, which is what is needed. In western states there are AP courses, but if a student wants to take the class and is not necessarily qualified, the student can still get into the class. They don't try to be as grade oriented. I'm not sure the school in the west prepares students for the rigor that would be expected and involved with an east coast Ivy League school. The students in the east are more prepared for the rigor.

I say east and west, but I'm really comparing the two schools I've taught at and the experiences I've had.

Other Education Environments
Have not really considered teaching in other education environments. Homeschooling doesn't interest me even though I have children of my own. I like coming to work; it's a nice break.

The idea of strictly tutoring is very appealing many days. The area I live in, a person can tutor every hour of every day and charge from $100 to $150 per hour. Monetarily it makes sense, but I'm not sure I want to have the same students all the time. Also, if you're not intentionally proactive, tutoring can turn into a time where students simply do their homework with you. Tutoring should be a time for extra help and not just doing homework. One main reason I wouldn't consider it is because of benefits.

Public school I would never consider anymore. At this stage in my life, I don't want to go back and get a teaching certificate. In my bias opinion, if I had to sit through a class on how to manage or decorate my classroom or how to rearrange my desk, I would go mad. I don't believe this is what I need to focus on.

I'm very happy in private schools and this is where I want to be. I went to public school and got a great education. However, having children of my own changes one's perspective and I prefer my children be in a private school setting.

Driving Factors

Funny you should ask. Don't tell my mother, but in my 4th year of engineering school, I knew I wasn't interested in engineering. I knew I wanted to teach. After graduation, I got a job teaching at a public school and called my parents to tell them about the job. At the time, I planned to go back and get my teaching certificate. I distinctly remember my mother asking me why I would go through four years of engineering school to be a teacher, because those who can do, those who can't teach.

I was completely taken aback. She's my mom, so I thought she was right. I called the school and said I'm really sorry, but I'm not going to be able to accept the offer. I found an engineering job and for the next year I was miserable. I called my mom and told her I hated the job, started applying for other jobs and began looking at public schools.

It happened there was a private school on the east coast looking to hire a math teacher. I was lucky; I fell into the position. For the school to hire somebody with no teaching experience to teach a math course was a big stretch. The head of the math department felt he saw a good teacher in me, took a chance and it worked out. I haven't looked back. The choice of public versus private was what I fell into and teaching in a private school environment is what I love.

Challenges You Encountered

I don't believe there are any challenges I've had to consider. Regarding teaching math, I simply knew how to do it. The first three years involved a lot of fine-tuning and figuring out how to teach someone else. That would probably be the biggest challenge, trying to figure out how to make that transition between me knowing it and understanding it and how to communicate it to a group of high school students.

I've had opportunities and experiences to teach on the east coast, west coast and in between. Finding a job as a high school math teacher has been very easy for me in the private sector.

Obstacles to Overcome

This one pops up depending on the student and the year, but one of the biggest obstacles is the parent. When you work at a private school where it costs over $20,000 a year to send a child, it seems some parents think they're actually buying the education; buying the grade. When their child is in a class they probably shouldn't be in and earning a grade lower than what the parents would like, things can get nasty, quick. That's the biggest obstacle.

For the most part, the schools I've worked at, my fellow teachers and the administration have been very supportive. Most of the time when there are issues with parents, it's not just with you. The issues had come up in previous years with previous teachers and are mainly repeat offenders. I teach juniors and seniors, so by the time these students are in my classes, I've heard the issues and am somewhat familiar with what to expect.

Benefits You Received
One of the major benefits is my children are able to attend the same school I teach at and we receive reduced tuition. For me that's a major benefit.

As I previously stated, the professional development I have access to and is made available is out of this world. I sign up to go to a conference; it gets approved and includes flight, hotel, and expenses. This is really nice.

Benefit to Others
It's nice to have students come back and tell me they took a math course in college and it was so easy. They had gotten an "A" and were tutoring others. It's always nice to hear things like this. Several students have gone on to study math, but I prefer to not get too attached to any of my students. I like them and I think they're great, but I don't develop Facebook friendships. I keep boundaries in that I'm the teacher, they're the student and I'm here to teach. The experiences I have with students when they're in school are great and awesome, but once they graduate, I go on.

It can be difficult, especially for younger teachers, to draw a line and keep the teacher-student relationship from becoming a friendship. The social media platforms enable teachers to create groups for their classes. It's so easy to get sucked into the social aspect of school and what's happening outside of school. If a student is struggling with something or has problems at home and needs somebody to confide in, I would be there to listen. However, I don't go out of my way as I prefer to keep relationships professional and at school.

The major benefit to others is I believe my students learn, they know I am the teacher and they learn to respect that professional relationship.

Social Challenges

Bullying happens regardless of where you are and now it even happens online. It's devastating as children can be so mean to each other. We've had children leave school because they felt they couldn't have any friends. No school is immune from drinking and drugs and I believe some of our students have tried both, to some degree. Also, vaping and juuling are bringing smoking back in a new way along with other associated dangers.

I have seen some alcohol issues in school. In my many years of teaching, I've seen a few cases or instances where students either take drugs prior to coming to school or are drinking at school. It's not a huge problem and I'm confident it's less than what you find in a large public school. When it's a small private school and one or two students are known for doing these things, it seems like it's a huge problem.

The administration prefers to keep incidents private and that's a source of contention between teachers and administrators. They want to protect the students and not have reputations marred or ruined. Many times in private schools, you can buy your way out of getting in trouble, which is a horrible thing to say. But, this is no surprise and I've seen it happen.

Changes to Consider

It would be nice for faculty, administration, parents and even students to be willing to adjust and change more readily. Particularly with older teachers, they get stuck in a rut and will tell you this is the way they do it, this is the way they've always done it and this is the way they're going to do it. Yet, sometimes things don't work and everything isn't always black and white. I didn't necessarily enjoy all the talking we did in the west, but there is a place for it. For example, many schools take the top down approach, where the administration makes the decisions and tell the teachers. There are times when teachers have great ideas and more collaboration could benefit everyone.

It would be nice to have more openness. Some parents see their child gets an "A" in math in the 8th, 9th and 10th grades and then gets a "B" in the 11th grade and it's assumed the teacher is at fault. The fact is things shift and change and things happen for the better or for the worse. Ironically, education is always changing while those in education don't seem to change.

Closing Remarks

Teaching is a great lifestyle and I really enjoy it. It's interesting and teaching can be very rewarding. You can feel great about it and have a wonderful month. You can have a class where everybody understands what's going on and everything is going smoothly. You can be flying high and then all of a sudden one parent comes in and brings you down very quickly. Nevertheless, that's life.

In some ways, teaching is like a house of cards. You can be feeling great, but it's pretty easy to get knocked down. Fortunately, it's easy to rebuild a house of cards and feel great again.

My final cents:

Unfortunately, many people believe all private schools are too expensive and families can't afford the tuition as well as the additional expenses. This is the case for the school Annie teaches at. However, many private schools and academies have students that represent a diverse population and come from low-socioeconomic families. The majority of parents simply seek an education environment that will provide a quality education for their child.

Like many states, this state offers various scholarships and tax credit programs. A few states have authorized education savings accounts or ESAs for K-12. These programs were created to give parents choice for seeking the best education environment for their child. Though not all private schools in all states accept state legislated programs, don't automatically discount a school.

Many people pontificate about ensuring all children receive a quality education and sending a child to a private school increases the probability. I believe education is a business and when a business doesn't provide a quality service, they typically don't stay in business very long. Yes, administrators change, teachers change and curriculum changes. However, I believe it's more about having engaged parents that are the driving entity to ensure quality is part of the equation. They need to establish expectations and demand results. Regardless of ones' economic status, consumers want value for their hard earned dollars. Competition is good and competition in education should be no different.

Math positions in K-12 education can be difficult to fill. There are many people who have been brainwashed over the years to believe math is too difficult. Math may not be easy to understand for some, but math is probably the most logical subject to learn. There are rules, formulas, constants, equations, etc. that follow a logical flow. I believe math seems to be difficult for many because of the way it is taught, not because it is a difficult subject.

During a visit to a local public school, I spoke to several students in a technical design class. The young lady I spoke with said she really liked the class, was glad she was able to get into it that year and began to show me some of what she had learned. However, what resonated with me is just before I left she reiterated she really liked the class and it has even helped her in math. You see, when students are able to apply what they need to learn, it becomes real and meaningful. When teachers engage their students in an activity or project, students see results, learn better and retain information.

Recommendations:

Parents who have a child struggling in their current education environment should research what options they have in their local area. There is the local public school where the address dictates the school their child will attend. There are typically at least one or two private schools in the area. Homeschooling is always an option. However, I would recommend visiting the state's Department of Education website. I believe this should be the first place to look, because parents will find what programs are authorized within their state.

When parents are seeking alternative education environments, make inquiries about various funding options. You may be surprised at what the school offers or who they can refer you to for financial solutions.

Sacrifice is a word not used very often in today's society. However, if a parent wants to ensure their child receives a quality education in the best environment for them, sacrifices have to be made. We all can look at cutting back on something in order to provide our child that desired quality. Don't buy that third TV for the house or eat out four nights a week or buy numerous video games. We've all heard that *education is the great equalizer*. So regardless of your current economic status; set a goal, make a plan and you will find you can afford more than you think. Invest in your child!

Concluding Notes:

Review the state constitution to see what authorized programs are in the state you live. There will be either state codes or state statutes that will provide further information regarding legislated programs and the affiliated policy.

Each state has a Department of Education. Some have more consumer friendly websites then others. Whether you are looking for public, private or homeschool information, this is the first place to seek information relevant to your state.

One of the easiest ways to find information today is by searching the Internet. There are many organizations that support a variety of education options. The parent simply needs to decide what is best for their child and then search, seek, speak to others and you will find a solution.

Conclusion

It has been such a privilege to meet and speak with these individuals. Each one brings their own perspective to the world of education based on their involvement, what they have dealt with, experienced and what the state they live in legally allows. All of these individuals are courageous, exceptional and remarkable for telling their stories.

I trust each one provides an element of support and strength to some who may be, or knows of someone, dealing with a similar situation. Though these stories may not be unique in what they convey, they are personal.

In our current environment of political correctness, it is difficult to speak out against the behemoth bureaucracies at the federal, state and local levels, which have been in existence for over 200+ years. We all have obstacles, which prevents us from adequately recognizing and assessing perceived barriers when it comes to education. While parents should have the freedom to choose an education environment that is right for their child and best meets their individual needs, there are many reasons this is not the case.

Not long ago I was participating in a writing group where a picture prompt of a Swiss knife was shown. We were asked to write about how this relates to our topic. My first thought was education and Swiss knife have a common theme: *there are many tools within one system.* The tools in the knife can be used to accomplish a variety of results. In the same vein, the education system has many tools to help students learn, achieve desired results and produce specific outcomes.

Because there are many tools in the education toolbox, I believe there is much work that can be done to improve outcomes. Opportunities abound when it comes to shaping an education system to meet the countless needs of our children for a 21st century workforce.

Our nation has educated millions since our founding fathers declared our independence in 1776 and signed our constitution in 1787, when they created our constitutional republic. In 1979, President Carter decided at the end of his term to create a U.S. Department of Education. This agency has become another behemoth bureaucracy that provides overarching policy and unfunded regulatory mandates that garner limited value to education. Was a Secretary level department necessary? I'll leave that to you, the reader, to decide. As for myself, I advocate for ending the U.S. Department of Education (DoED), as we know it today.

Thinking about possible solutions to move forward, I offer a couple. The first solution, at a minimum, would be to designate the department to an Agency and house it within the U.S. Department of Labor. The primary purpose of the DoED is to gather information and provide statistical data. These actions are duplicative efforts and align with the mission of the Bureau of Labor Statistics.

I would ensure the agency reduced its regulatory control at the federal level and relegate accountability and responsibility to the states, which is where it should be. Education has never been a right under the U.S. Constitution, it is a state issue and state constitutions consign education as a right. Allow states and local school districts to set standards and be accountable to the public.

The second change would be to rethink funding related to our education system. Eliminating the taxing authority to fund education would help improve school performance. When parents are in control of the funds, competition would drive decision-making, which in turn typically improves services. If performance is not at a level expected by the parent, then they will seek an alternative service provider. This could eliminate, or at least minimize, the external influencers that seek merely to retain power and control over the system.

If some level of government funding stays in place, then provide an education credit, deduction or allowance against income tax for parents to educate their children. This can shift the decision-making out of the hands of individuals who don't have a vested interest. When elected officials, lobbyists and unions drive the narrative and use public tax dollars to achieve their goals and objectives, this ultimately reveals the truth: *those who hold the purse strings, have the power and control.*

Let's consider: if funding the U.S. Department of Education were eliminated, how much money would be saved? It could be as much as $68billion, because this was their annual budget in 2016 and I'm sure it's only grown in the last four years. In addition, working parents would retain more of the money they earn and realize larger paychecks. This change enables parents to shop for and choose the education environment that best meets their child's needs.

When we hear politicians say *free education,* do people really believe it's *free?* Using public money as a funding source, far too many do equate this to *free* and do not connect the dots. However, someone is footing the bill and that someone is the American taxpayer. There is no such thing as a *free lunch* and this is also true for education.

Yes, there are many advantages to having an education, just as there are advantages to having a Swiss knife. However, the way we view and use these tools will determine the future of education in the United States. We cannot continue to do the same thing over and over and expect different results. This *is* the definition of *insanity*. It's essential we interject more common sense and less insanity into the system.

Regardless of your stance on the current education system, I believe we all can agree that some degree of change is necessary. Whether constitutional rights, funding considerations or regulations spur change, one thing must be a major component in the equation: *parents must have the freedom to decide the best education environment for their child.*

Endnotes

1. Abbott, Sarah. (2018). Interview conducted and recorded via phone on June 13, 2018.
2. Ali-Coleman, K. (2014). Mom jailed for enrolling kids in school tells her story in new book, film. Ebony Online. Retrieved from http://www.ebony.com/news-views/mom-jailed-for-enrolling-kids-in-school-tells-her-story-in-new-book-film-405#axzz50WQ16ks7.
3. Angle, Valarie. (2018). Interview conducted and recorded at Roanoke Library, Roanoke, VA on January 31, 2018.
4. Annie (Anonymous). (2018). Interview conducted and recorded via phone on March 12, 2018.
5. Blanks, Walter. (2018). Interview conducted and recorded via phone on February 26, 2018.
6. Care.com. (2018). 8 helpful special needs organizations. Retrieved from https://www.care.com/c/stories/6620/10-helpful-special-needs-organizations/.
7. Center for Education Reform. (2019). Choice and Charter Schools. Retrieved from https://www.edreform.com/issues/choice-charter-schools/advocacy/.
8. Channing, A & Tanglao, L. (2011). Ohio mom Kelley Williams-Bolar jailed for sending kids to better school district. ABC News Online. Retrieved from http://abcnews.go.com/US/ohio-mom-jailed-sending-kids-school-district/story?id=12763654.
9. Classical Conversations. (2019). Retrieved from https://www.classicalconversations.com.

10. EdChoice. (2018). The ABC's of school choice. Retrieved from https://www.edchoice.org.
11. EdChoice: Ohio. (2018). Retrieved from https://www.edchoice.org/school-choice/state/ohio/.
12. Education Improvement Scholarships Tax Credit Program (EISTC). (2013). Virginia Department of Education. Retrieved from http://www.doe.virginia.gov/school_finance/scholarships_tax_credits/index.shtml.
13. Florida Constitution. (2018). Retrieved from http://www.flsenate.gov/Laws/Constitution.
14. Florida Department of Education. (2018). Private School Directory. Tallahassee, Florida. Retrieved from http://www.fldoe.org.
15. Florida Department of Education. (2018). K-12 Public Schools: School Choice. Tallahassee, Florida. Retrieved from http://www.fldoe.org.
16. Florida Statute XLVIII (2019). K-20 education code; Chapters 1000–1013. Retrieved from http://www.leg.state.fl.us/statutes/.
17. Home Educators Association of Virginia (HEAV). (2018). Retrieved from https://heav.org.
18. Home School Legal Defense Association (HSLDA). (2018). Retrieved from https://hslda.org/content/.
19. Homeschooling in Virginia. (2018). Retrieved from http://www.homeschoolinginvirginia.com.
20. Individuals with Disabilities Education Act (IDEA). (1990). Retrieved from https://sites.ed.gov/idea/#.
21. Kapatoes, Melissa. Interview conducted and recorded in Viera, FL on March 23, 2018.

22. Keaton, Jeff. Interview conducted and recorded at Renewanation in Vinton, VA on May 3, 2018.

23. Luddy, Robert. Interview conducted and recorded at CaptiveAire in Raleigh, North Carolina on February 7, 2018.

24. Martin, M. (2011). Mother jailed for school fraud, flares controversy. National Public Radio (NPR) Online. Retrieved from https://www.npr.org/2011/01/28/133306180/Mother-Jailed-For-School-Fraud-Flares-Controversy.

25. Massachusetts Constitution. (2018). Retrieved from https://malegislature.gov/Laws/Constitution#chapterVSectionI.

26. Massachusetts Department of Education. (2018). Malden, MA. Retrieved from http://www.doe.mass.edu.

27. Massachusetts General Laws. (2018). Part 1, Title XI, Ch. 69-78A. Retrieved from https://malegislature.gov/Laws/GeneralLaws/PartI.

28. Merriweather, Denisha. Interview conducted and recorded in Washington, DC on June 20, 2018.

29. National School Choice Week. (2020). Retrieved from https://schoolchoiceweek.com.

30. North Carolina Constitution. (1971). Article XI Education. Retrieved from https://www.ncleg.gov/Laws/Constitution/Article9.

31. North Carolina Department of Public Instruction. (2019). Retrieved from https://www.dpi.nc.gov.

32. North Carolina General Statutes. (2019). Chapter 115 Elementary and Secondary Education. Retrieved from https://www.ncleg.gov/Laws/GeneralStatutesTOC.

33. Ohio Code. (2019). Title [33] XXXIII Education – Libraries. Retrieved from http://codes.ohio.gov/orc/33.

34. Ohio Constitution. (2018). Retrieved from https://www.legislature.ohio.gov/laws/ohio-constitution.

35. Ohio Department of Education. (2018). EdChoice Scholarship Program. Retrieved from http://education.ohio.gov/Topics/Other-Resources/Scholarships/EdChoice-Scholarship-Program.

36. Ohio Department of Education. (2018). Quality School Choice. Retrieved from https://education.ohio.gov/Topics/Quality-School-Choice.

37. O'Leary, J. D., Partin, E. L. & Speranza, B. (2011). What's not being said in the Williams-Bolar case? Thomas B. Fordham Institute. Retrieved from https://edexcellence.net/articles/whats-not-being-said-in-the-williams-bolar-case.

38. Parcells, Gina. Interview conducted and recorded at Hampton Roads Airport, Hampton, VA on May 4, 2018.

39. Ramaker, Michelle. Interview conducted and recorded at Eastlake Community Church, Moneta, VA on June 6, 2018.

40. Renewanation. (2019). Retrieved from https://www.renewanation.org.

41. School Choice Ohio. (2018). Retrieved from https://scohio.org.

42. Smith, Lorie. Interview conducted and recorded in Moneta, VA on May 14, 2018.

43. Smith Mountain Lake Christian Academy (SMLCA). (2019). Retrieved from https://www.smlca.org.
44. Step Up for Students. (2019). Scholarships in Florida. Retrieved from https://www.stepupforstudents.org.
45. Thales Academy (2019). Retrieved from https://www.thalesacademy.org.
46. The Organization of Virginia Homeschoolers. (2018). Retrieved from https://vahomeschoolers.org.
47. Time4Learning. (2018). Retrieved from https://www.time4learning.com.
48. U.S. Department Education. (2018). National Centers for Education Statistics (NCES). Retrieved from https://nces.ed.gov.
49. Virginia Code. (2019). Title 22.1 Education. Retrieved from https://law.lis.virginia.gov/vacode/title22.1/.
50. Virginia Constitution. (1971). Title VIII Education. Retrieved from https://law.lis.virginia.gov/constitution/.
51. Virginia Council of Private Education (VCPE). (2018). Retrieved from https://www.vcpe.org.
52. Virginia Department of Education. (2019). Retrieved from http://www.doe.virginia.gov.
53. Williams-Bolar, Kelley. Interview conducted and recorded via phone on February 19, 2018.